Poems of Andrew Marvell

POEMS OF
ANDREW MARVELL

Introduction by C. V. Wedgwood

The Folio Society

London 1964

The text of this edition is based on
The Poems and Letters of Andrew Marvell
edited by H. M. Margoliouth
by kind permission of the Clarendon Press, Oxford

PRINTED IN GREAT BRITAIN

*Printed and bound by W & J Mackay & Co Ltd, Chatham
Set in Van Dijck 11 point*

Contents

Introduction   7
A Dialogue between the Resolved Soul, and
   Created Pleasure   17
On a Drop of Dew   21
The Coronet   23
Eyes and Tears   24
Bermudas   27
Clorinda and Damon   29
A Dialogue between Thyrsis and Dorinda   30
A Dialogue between the Soul and Body   32
The Nymph complaining for the death of her Faun   34
Young Love   38
To his Coy Mistress   40
The unfortunate Lover   42
The Gallery   45
The Fair Singer   48
Mourning   49
Daphnis and Chloe   51
The Definition of Love   56
The Picture of little T. C. in a Prospect of Flowers   58
The Match   60
The Mower against Gardens   62
Damon the Mower   64
The Mower to the Glo-Worms   68
The Mower's Song   69
Ametas and Thestylis making Hay-Ropes   71
Musicks Empire   72
The Garden   74
An Epitaph upon ——   77
Upon the Hill and Grove at Bill-borow. To the
   Lord Fairfax   78

Contents

Upon Appleton House, to my Lord Fairfax   81
Fleckno, an English Priest at Rome   109
An Horatian Ode upon Cromwel's Return from
    Ireland   115
Tom May's Death   119
To his worthy Friend Doctor Witty upon his
    Translation of the Popular Errors   123
The Character of Holland   125
The First Anniversary of the Government under
    O. C.   130
On the Victory obtained by Blake over the
    Spaniards, in the Bay of Sanctacruze, in the Island
    of Teneriff. 1657   142
Two Songs at the Marriage of the Lord Fauconberg
    and the Lady Mary Cromwell   148
A Poem upon the Death of O. C.   153
On Mr Milton's Paradise Lost   163
Notes   165

Introduction

Andrew Marvell was born in 1621 and died in 1678. His life thus coincides with an epoch of bitter political and religious division among his countrymen and of startling changes in the fortunes of the nation. He saw the peaceful decade of King Charles I, when he was a young scholar-poet at Cambridge; this was followed by the distress and disaster of the Civil Wars. Then came the national resurgence and the era of victory under the austere rule of Cromwell and, in his later years, the frivolity and indifference that marked the reign of Charles II.

Those poems of Marvell which we know and love best today were written in his earlier years before he had become involved in politics. Later, as a hard-working Civil Servant under Cromwell and as a member of Parliament under Charles II, he lost the inclination for the pastoral verses in which he had once delighted. Contemporaries thought of him not as a lyric poet but as a fearless and ferocious satirist of the political scene. A man of great integrity, he remained true to the Puritan virtues and Cromwellian policies that he had come to admire in his early maturity. He was known in his own time for his stately verses on the glories of Oliver Cromwell, and his attacks on Charles II, not for the lines he wrote on the death of King Charles I. Both his life and his posthumous reputation are full of contradictions.

Andrew Marvell was the son of an Anglican clergyman in Yorkshire who became headmaster of the grammar school at Hull a few years after the poet was born. Young Marvell was intelligent and must have been precocious, since he proceeded from his father's school to Cambridge before he was thirteen. At Cambridge he wrote occasional

7

elegant verses both in English and in Latin, but very little is known of his career. During the Civil War he went abroad, travelling in France, Italy, Spain and Holland. He must presumably have undertaken this long and expensive tour as the tutor and companion of some wealthy young gentleman, as he would not himself have had a large enough fortune to defray his expenses.

On his return to England our knowledge of his career becomes more definite. He was for about two years tutor to Mary Fairfax, the only child of Lord Fairfax, head of one of the greatest families in Yorkshire and famous throughout the country as the commander-in-chief of that Army which had defeated the King in the Civil War and brought him to the scaffold. Both the Army and the power that went with it had, by the time of Marvell's return, fallen into the hands of Oliver Cromwell, once Lieutenant-General under Fairfax. Fairfax himself, more perturbed than gratified by the outcome of his victories, had now retired to his splendid mansion of Nun Appleton in Yorkshire. It was here that Marvell, in the intervals of instructing the young heiress, composed many of his loveliest poems on rural and on garden themes. It must have been here on a still day in summer that he saw a Yorkshire Ametas and Thestylis making hay-ropes, and watched the rhythmic movements of the mowers in the meadows which no less than three times inspired his verses. It was certainly here, in the well-stocked, well-tended gardens of Appleton House, that he contemplated the troubles through which his country had passed and, with a wry sweetness, compared the formal planting of Lord Fairfax's flowerbeds to the disciplined ranks of an army.

Unhappy! shall we never more
That sweet Militia restore,

When Gardens only had their Towrs,
And all the Garrisons were Flowrs,
When Roses only Arms might bear,
And Men did rosie Garlands wear?
Tulips, in several Colours barr'd,
Were then the Switzers of our Guard.

His capacities entitled him to something better than a tutor's place. In 1653 John Milton, who was then 'secretary in the foreign tongues' to the Republican Government, required an assistant. He probably remembered Marvell from Cambridge days. At any rate, he wrote to the Council of State strongly recommending him for the appointment. He described him as 'a man both by report and by the conversation I have had with him of singular desert for the State to make use of. He hath spent four years abroad in Holland, France, Italy and Spain to very good purpose, as I believe, and the gaining of those four languages. Besides he is a scholar and well read in the latin and Greek authors. It would be hard to find a man so fit every way as this gentleman.'

In spite of this testimonial the Council of State had other ideas, and Marvell had to go back to tutoring. This time he was put in charge of a boy at Eton who happened to be the ward of Oliver Cromwell. This connection brought him into personal touch with the Lord Protector and his Court. In 1657 he was at length appointed assistant to Milton. This relatively brief connection with Cromwell and his Government aroused in Marvell a sincere and wholehearted admiration to which he remained faithful until the day of his death.

We have very little evidence of his earlier political sympathies or his religious outlook. He once described his father as a loyal conformist to the rituals of the

9

Church of England 'though none of the most over-
running or eager in them'. His youthful background was
therefore loyal to the Government of Charles I, but with
a leaning towards Protestant simplicity, not to say
austerity. His early poems, and his long absence from
England during the war, suggest a contemplative, almost
a quietist frame of mind.

> *How vainly men themselves amaze*
> *To win the Palm, the Oke, or Bayes . . .*

he wrote. He preferred to meditate upon the infinite,
mirrored in the delicate and fertile beauty of the natural
world

> *Annihilating all that's made*
> *To a green Thought in a green Shade.*

Thus, when he returned to England at the end of the
Civil War, he looked upon the terrible happenings of the
last years and even upon the King's death as though he
was a spectator at some Greek or Roman tragedy. Some
have tried to prove his sympathies with the Royalists
from his earlier verses and especially from the famous
Horatian Ode upon Cromwel's Return from Ireland. (Inciden-
tally this magnificent poem, though evidently written in
1650, was unknown to contemporaries, was suppressed in
the first posthumous edition of Marvell's poems in 1681,
and only became public property when it was published
in 1776.)

The poem offers a distant and at times faintly cynical
homage to Cromwell while including what is by now the
most famous of all poetic tributes to the noble dignity of
the King. But there is a world of difference between Marvell's attitude and the passionate (and largely forgotten)
effusions of Royalist poets on the death of Charles—those

of Cowley for instance, or Cleveland or Henry King.
Marvell is not pierced to the heart; he is not aghast. He is
moved and impressed, as any sensitive spectator would
be, at a great tragic play. He even uses the word 'actor'
for the King, a phrase which a true Royalist would have
rejected as impious.

> That thence the Royal Actor born
> The Tragick Scaffold might adorn:
> > While round the armed Bands
> > Did clap their bloody hands.

> He nothing common did or mean
> Upon that memorable Scene:
> > But with his keener Eye
> > The Axes edge did try:

> Nor call'd the Gods with vulgar spight,
> To vindicate his helpless Right?
> > But bow'd his comely Head
> > Down as upon a Bed.

Five years later, after he had come into the circle of
the Lord Protector, he published, anonymously, his poem
On the First Anniversary of the Government under O.C. From
this poem it is clear that he felt a genuine gratitude and
admiration for the man who had imposed peace on the
war-torn nation and had restored, with almost incredible
speed, her international and naval reputation. The contemplative Marvell of the earlier poems had become
politically 'committed' and was to remain so. Of all the
elegies on Cromwell's death, Marvell's alone speaks the
language of genuine personal grief. The young Dryden
and the veteran Waller shed poetic tears in great abun-
dance on Cromwell's bier, and two years later crowned

the returning King with garlands of adulatory verse. Not so Marvell. He accepted the restored monarchy, was returned to Parliament for Hull and served the constituents faithfully in the House of Commons. But he remained undeviating in his faith to Protestant and Cromwellian policies, and he bitterly deplored the corruption of government at home and the collapse of English prestige abroad which followed the Restoration.

His integrity and the quiet austerity of his personal life earned him respect, and he never ceased to be a lively, well-informed and interesting companion. Although, as Aubrey tells us, 'he had not a general acquaintance', he was always popular among intelligent and discriminating men, whatever their political opinions. Aubrey has left us an attractive picture of him: 'He was of middling stature, pretty strong sett, roundish faced, cherry cheek't, hazell eie, browne haire.' His reputation as a discriminating literary critic also seems to have stood high, and the praise which he accorded to such poets as Rochester and Samuel Butler for the sharpness of their satire shows that he could appreciate wit and good verses whether or not he approved of the opinions expressed.

His reputation enabled him to do good service to his old master John Milton, who was in serious danger at the Restoration because of his writings against the late King. While Milton was in hiding, Marvell worked up a party for him in the House of Commons so that he gained the full benefit of the Royal pardon.

During the last eighteen years of his life Marvell sat in Parliament, sending home regular reports to his constituents and writing letters to friends which have been invaluable to historians of this epoch. Once he was absent for over a year when he was on the staff of the English ambassador to Sweden, Denmark and Russia.

Otherwise he lived quietly in London, turning his poetic talent to a new use. He became the most virulent of the anti-Court satirists. Most of this work was circulated anonymously, but Marvell's authorship was often known, and his reputation was such that the work of other writers was often passed off as his.

Samuel Pepys read his ferocious poem on the mismanagement of the Dutch War and the disaster in the Medway, and set down in his diary: 'it made my heart ache to read, it being too sharp, and so true.' Small wonder that when Marvell died it was rumoured that the 'Jesuits' had poisoned him to silence the dangerous pen which attacked the pro-French and Catholic policies of the Court. In fact Marvell died, like so many others at this time, through the ineptitude of a doctor who applied the wrong remedies to a slight fever. He was buried in St Giles's in the Fields, and his admirers may still see his monument and pause among the din of London traffic to remember the contemplative sweetness of his poetry.

At his death, and for many years afterwards, he was famous exclusively for his fierce political satire. But nothing dates more than satire. The quarrels are now dead. The most telling of his bitter jokes need a whole battery of footnotes by way of explanation, and for this reason the *Satires* are not included in this edition. Over the long years his fame as a satirist faded, to be replaced slowly but surely by his fame as a true poet. The earlier poems were published shortly after his death, but did not at first achieve popularity. Marvell's complex metaphysical conceits and his metrical experiments had little appeal in the time of Dryden and Pope.

But in the nineteenth century Charles Lamb would speak affectionately of him, and in the twentieth century his reputation has steadily risen. The themes of his poetry

are simple and classical—the fleeting character of human
joys, the perishable sweetness of the natural world about
us. Sometimes, as in *Bermudas,* there is an undercurrent of
Christian faith. More often the tone has a classical
melancholy. He had a peculiarly sensitive ear, and often
the theme of his poem governs the rhythm. So in *Bermudas* we feel the gentle pulsation of the oars and in *The
Mower's Song* the sweep of the scythe. In the *Coy Mistress,*
perhaps the most famous of all today, it is not fanciful to
hear the quickening pace of *Times winged Charriot hurrying
near.* This poem makes its impact through an apparently
playful wit, an elaborately worked out series of conceits
that make us smile—

> *My vegetable Love should grow
> Vaster then Empires, and more slow.*

In the midst of this teasing humour the bleak lines—

> *And yonder all before us lye
> Desarts of vast Eternity*

make a sudden startling contrast. Human beings may
laugh at their condition, but it is in truth no laughing
matter.

This is one of the oldest themes of poetry, and Marvell
borrowed from classical sources—from Horace, from
Catullus—in his treatment of it. But he gave to it something peculiarly English. It is not merely that his gardens
and fields are as English as Shakespeare's. There is also a
peculiarly English quality about his wit—the extrava-
gance of his imaginings in the *Coy Mistress* has almost an
Edward Lear touch. Mingled with this mocking extrava-
gance, so often a feature of English comedy from Ben
Jonson to Thackeray and Lewis Carroll, there is also a
deliberate and very English understatement. He gets his

effects by the merest glancing allusion. *Desarts of vast Eternity* he writes, starting a shudder in our minds, and then resumes his teasing-wooing again in a lighter tone. So also with *The Picture of Little T.C.* and *The Nymph complaining for the Death of her Faun*, the underlying tragedy, the brevity and sorrow of human life are indicated only by a touch. In this understatement he seems very much our compatriot, just as in the permanence of his themes he is always our contemporary.

There is in Marvell at his best a warmth, a love of colour and beauty, a true feeling for the natural loveliness of the world that must appeal to every sensitive ear and eye. But the shadows that fall across his landscape remind us of the ephemeral nature of human happiness, the shortness of life and of the troubled and divided world in which Marvell himself lived and wrote.

A Dialogue between the Resolved Soul, and Created Pleasure

Courage my Soul, now learn to wield
The weight of thine immortal Shield.
Close on thy Head thy Helmet bright.
Ballance thy Sword against the Fight.
See where an Army, strong as fair,
With silken Banners spreads the air.
Now, if thou bee'st that thing Divine,
In this day's Combat let it shine:
And shew that Nature wants an Art
To conquer one resolved heart.

Pleasure

Welcome the Creations Guest,
Lord of Earth, and Heavens Heir.
Lay aside that Warlike Crest,
And of Nature's banquet share:
Where the Souls of fruits and flow'rs
Stand prepar'd to heighten yours.

Soul

I sup above, and cannot stay
To bait so long upon the way.

Pleasure

On these downy Pillows lye,
Whose soft Plumes will thither fly:
On these Roses strow'd so plain
Lest one Leaf thy Side should strain.

The Resolved Soul, and Created Pleasure

Soul

My gentler Rest is on a Thought,
Conscious of doing what I ought.

Pleasure

If thou bee'st with Perfumes pleas'd,
Such as oft the Gods appeas'd,
Thou in fragrant Clouds shalt show
Like another God below.

Soul

A Soul that knowes not to presume
Is Heaven's and its own perfume.

Pleasure

Every thing does seem to vie
Which should first attract thine Eye:
But since none deserves that grace,
In this Crystal view *thy* face.

Soul

When the Creator's skill is priz'd,
The rest is all but* Earth disguis'd.

Pleasure

Heark how Musick then prepares
For thy Stay these charming Aires;
Which the posting Winds recall,
And suspend the Rivers Fall.

Soul

Had I but any time to lose,
On this I would it all dispose.

The Resolved Soul, and Created Pleasure

Cease Tempter. None can chain a mind
Whom this sweet Chordage cannot bind.

Chorus

Earth cannot shew so brave a Sight
As when a single Soul does fence
The Batteries* of alluring Sense,
And Heaven views it with delight.
  Then persevere: for still new Charges sound:
  And if thou overcom'st thou shalt be crown'd.

Pleasure

All this fair, and soft, and sweet,
  Which scatteringly doth shine,
Shall within one Beauty meet,
  And she be only thine.

Soul

If things of Sight such Heavens be,
What Heavens are those we cannot see?

Pleasure

Where so e're thy Foot shall go
  The minted Gold shall lie;
Till thou purchase all below,
  And want new Worlds to buy.

Soul

Wer't not a price who'ld value Gold?
And that's worth nought that can be sold.

Pleasure

Wilt thou all the Glory have
  That War or Peace commend?

Half the World shall be thy Slave
 The other half thy Friend.

Soul

What Friends, if to my self untrue?
What Slaves, unless I captive you?

Pleasure

Thou shalt know each hidden Cause;
 And see the future Time:
Try what depth the Center* draws;
 And then to Heaven climb.

Soul

None thither mounts by the degree
Of Knowledge, but Humility.*

Chorus

Triumph, triumph, victorious Soul;
The World has not one Pleasure more:
The rest does lie beyond the Pole,
And is thine everlasting Store.

On a Drop of Dew

See how the Orient Dew,
Shed from the Bosom of the Morn
   Into the blowing Roses,
Yet careless of its Mansion new;
For* the clear Region where 'twas born
   Round in its self incloses.*
   And in its little Globes Extent,
Frames as it can its native Element.*
    How it the purple flow'r does slight,
      Scarce touching where it lyes,
    But gazing back upon the Skies,
      Shines with a mournful Light;
        Like its own Tear,
Because so long divided from the Sphear.
    Restless it roules and unsecure,
      Trembling lest it grow impure:
  Till the warm Sun pitty it's Pain,
And to the Skies exhale it back again.
      So the Soul, that Drop, that Ray
Of the clear Fountain of Eternal Day,
Could it within the humane flow'r be seen,
    Remembring still its former height,
    Shuns the sweat leaves and blossoms green;
    And, recollecting* its own Light,
Does, in its pure and circling thoughts, express
The greater Heaven in an Heaven less.
    In how coy a Figure wound,
    Every way it turns away:
    So the World excluding round,*
    Yet receiving in the Day.
    Dark beneath, but bright above:

On a Drop of Dew

Here disdaining, there in Love,
How loose and easie hence to go:
How girt and ready to ascend.
Moving but on a point below,
It all about does upwards bend.
Such did the Manna's sacred Dew destil;
White, and intire, though congeal'd and chill.
Congeal'd on Earth:* but does, dissolving, run
Into the Glories of th' Almighty Sun.

The Coronet

When for the Thorns with which I long, too long,
   With many a piercing wound,
   My Saviours head have crown'd,
I seek with Garlands to redress that Wrong:
   Through every Garden, every Mead,
I gather flow'rs (my fruits are only flow'rs)
   Dismantling all the fragrant Towers*
That once adorn'd my Shepherdesses head.
And now when I have summ'd up all my store,
   Thinking (so I my self deceive)
   So rich a Chaplet thence to weave
As never yet the king of Glory wore:
   Alas I find the Serpent old
   That, twining in his speckled breast,
   About the flow'rs disguis'd does fold,
   With wreaths of Fame and interest.
Ah, foolish Man, that would'st debase with them,
And mortal Glory, Heavens Diadem!
But thou who only could'st the Serpent tame,
Either his slipp'ry knots at once untie,
And disentangle all his winding Snare:
Or shatter too with him my curious frame:*
And let these wither, so that he may die,
Though set with Skill and chosen out with Care.
That they, while Thou on both their Spoils dost tread,
May crown thy Feet, that could not crown thy Head.

Eyes and Tears

1

How wisely Nature did decree,
With the same Eyes to weep and see!
That, having view'd the object vain,
They might be ready to complain.

2

And, since the Self-deluding Sight,
In a false Angle takes each hight;
These Tears which better measure all,
Like wat'ry Lines and Plummets fall.

3

Two Tears, which Sorrow long did weigh
Within the Scales of either Eye,
And then paid out in equal Poise,
Are the true price of all my Joyes.

4

What in the World most fair appears,
Yea, even Laughter, turns to Tears:
And all the Jewels which we prize,
Melt in these Pendants of the Eyes.

5

I have through every Garden been,
Amongst the Red, the White, the Green;
And yet, from all the flow'rs I saw,
No Hony, but these Tears could draw.

6

So the all-seeing Sun each day
Distills the World with Chymick Ray;
But finds the Essence only Showers,
Which straight in pity back he powers.

7

Yet happy they whom Grief doth bless,
That weep the more, and see the less:
And, to preserve their Sight more true,
Bath still their Eyes in their own Dew.

8

So *Magdalen*, in Tears more wise
Dissolv'd those captivating Eyes,
Whose liquid Chaines could flowing meet
To fetter her Redeemers feet.

9

Not full sailes hasting loaden home,
Nor the chast Ladies pregnant Womb,
Nor *Cynthia* Teeming show's so fair,
As two Eyes swoln with weeping are.

10

The sparkling Glance that shoots Desire,
Drench'd in these Waves, does lose it fire.
Yea oft the Thund'rer pitty takes
And here the hissing Lightning slakes.

11

The Incense was to Heaven dear,
Not as a Perfume, but a Tear.

And Stars shew lovely in the Night,
But as they seem the Tears of Light.

12

Ope then mine Eyes your double Sluice,
And practise so your noblest Use.
For others too can see, or sleep;
But only humane Eyes can weep.

13

Now like two Clouds dissolving drop,
And at each Tear in distance stop:
Now like two Fountains trickle down:
Now like two floods o'return and drown.

14

Thus let your Streams o'reflow your Springs,
Till Eyes and Tears be the same things:
And each the other's difference bears;
These weeping Eyes, those seeing Tears.

Bermudas*

Where the remote *Bermudas* ride
In th' Oceans bosome unespy'd,
From a small Boat, that row'd along,
The listning Winds receiv'd this Song.
    What should we do but sing his Praise
That led us through the watry Maze,
Unto an Isle so long unknown,*
And yet far kinder than our own?
Where he the huge Sea-Monsters wracks,
That lift the Deep upon their Backs.*
He lands us on a grassy Stage;
Safe from the Storms, and Prelat's* rage.
He gave us this eternal Spring,
Which here enamells every thing;
And sends the Fowl's to us in care,
On daily Visits through the Air.
He hangs in shades the Orange bright,
Like golden Lamps in a green Night.
And does in the Pomgranates close,
Jewels more rich than *Ormus*　show's.
He makes the Figs our mouths to meet;
And throws the Melons at our feet.
But Apples* plants of such a price,
No Tree could ever bear them twice.
With Cedars, chosen by his hand,
From *Lebanon*, he stores the Land.
And makes the hollow Seas, that roar,
Proclaime the Ambergris on shoar.
He cast (of which we rather boast)
The Gospels Pearl upon our Coast.
And in these Rocks for us did frame

Bermudas

A Temple, where to sound his Name.
Oh, let our Voice his Praise exalt,
Till it arrive at Heavens Vault:
Which thence (perhaps) rebounding, may
Eccho beyond the *Mexique Bay*.
Thus sung they, in the *English* boat,
An holy and a chearful Note,
And all the way, to guide their Chime,
With falling Oars they kept the time.

Clorinda and Damon

C. *Damon* come drive thy flocks this way.
D. No: 'tis too late they went astray.
C. I have a grassy Scutcheon spy'd,
    Where *Flora* blazons all her pride.
    The Grass I aim to feast thy Sheep:
    The Flow'rs I for thy Temples keep.
D. Grass withers; and the Flow'rs too fade.
C. Seize the short Joyes then, ere they vade.
    Seest thou that unfrequented Cave?
D. That den? C. Loves Shrine. D. But Virtue's Grave.
C. In whose cool bosome we may lye
    Safe from the Sun. D. not Heaven's Eye.
C. Near this, a Fountaines liquid Bell
    Tinkles within the concave Shell.
D. Might a Soul bath there and be clean,
    Or slake its Drought? C. What is't you mean?
D. These once had been enticing things,
    Clorinda, Pastures, Caves, and Springs.
C. And what late change? D. The other day
    Pan met me. C. What did great *Pan* say?
D. Words that transcend poor Shepherds skill,
    But He ere since my Songs does fill:
    And his Name swells my slender Oate.
C. Sweet must *Pan* sound in *Damons* Note.
D. *Clorinda's* voice might make it sweet.
C. Who would not in *Pan's* Praises meet?

Chorus

Of Pan *the flowry Pastures sing,*
Caves eccho, and the Fountains ring.
Sing then while he doth us inspire:
For all the World is our Pan's *Quire.*

29

A Dialogue between Thyrsis and Dorinda

DORINDA When Death, shall part us from these Kids,
And shut up our divided Lids,
Tell me *Thyrsis*, prethee do,
Whither thou and I must go.

THYRSIS To the Elizium: (DORINDA) oh where i'st?
THYRSIS A Chast Soul, can never mis't.
DORINDA I know no way, but one, our home;
Is our cell Elizium?

THYRSIS Turn thine Eye to yonder Skie,
There the milky way doth lye;
'Tis a sure but rugged way,
That leads to Everlasting day.

DORINDA There Birds may nest, but how can I,
That have no wings and cannot fly?

THYRSIS Do not sigh (fair Nimph) for fire
Hath no wings, yet doth aspire
Till it hit, against the pole,
Heaven's the Center of the Soul.

DORINDA But in Elizium how do they
Pass Eternity away?

THYRSIS Oh, ther's, neither hope nor fear
Ther's no Wolf, no Fox, nor Bear.
No need of Dog to fetch our stray,
Our Lightfoot we may give away;
No Oat-pipe's needfull, there thine Ears
May feast with Musick of the Spheres.

30

A Dialogue between Thyrsis and Dorinda

DORINDA   Oh sweet! oh sweet! How I my future state
          By silent thinking, Antidate:
          I prethee let us spend our time to come
          In talking of *Elizium*.

THYRSIS   Then I'le go on: There, sheep are full
          Of sweetest grass, and softest wooll;
          There, birds sing Consorts, garlands grow,
          Cool winds do whisper, springs do flow.
          There, alwayes is, a rising Sun,
          And day is ever, but begun.
          Shepheards there, bear equal sway,
          And every Nimph's a Queen of *May*.

DORINDA   Ah me, ah me.

THYRSIS   *Dorinda*, why do'st Cry?

DORINDA   I'm sick, I'm sick, and fain would dye:
          Convince me now, that this is true;
          By bidding, with mee, all adieu.

THYRSIS   I cannot live, without thee, I
          Will for thee, much more with thee dye.

Chorus Then let us give *Carillo* charge o'th Sheep,
          And thou and I'le pick poppies and them steep
          In wine, and drink on't even till we weep,
          So shall we smoothly pass away in sleep.

31

A Dialogue between the Soul and Body

Soul

O who shall, from this Dungeon, raise
A Soul inslav'd so many wayes?
With bolts of Bones, that fetter'd stands
In Feet; and manacled in Hands.
Here blinded with an Eye; and there
Deaf with the drumming of an Ear.
A Soul hung up, as 'twere, in Chains
Of Nerves, and Arteries, and Veins.
Tortur'd, besides each other part,
In a vain Head, and double Heart.

Body

O who shall me deliver whole,
From bonds of this Tyrannic Soul?
Which, stretcht upright, impales me so,
That mine own Precipice I go;
And warms and moves this needless* Frame:
(A Fever could but do the same.)
And, wanting where its spight to try,
Has made me live to let me dye.
A Body that could never rest,
Since this ill Spirit it possest.

Soul

What Magick could me thus confine
Within anothers Grief to pine?
Where whatsoever it complain,
I feel, that cannot feel, the pain.
And all my Care its self employes,
That to preserve, which me destroys:

32

A Dialogue between the Soul and Body

Constrain'd not only to indure
Diseases, but, whats worse, the Cure:
And ready oft the Port to gain,
Am Shipwrackt into Health again.

Body

But Physick yet could never reach
The Maladies Thou me dost teach;
Whom first the Cramp of Hope does Tear:
And then the Palsie Shakes of Fear.
The Pestilence of Love does heat:
Or Hatred's hidden Ulcer eat.
Joy's chearful Madness does perplex:
Or Sorrow's other Madness vex.
Which Knowledge forces me to know;
And Memory will not foregoe.
What but a Soul could have the wit
To build me up for Sin so fit?
So Architects do square and hew,
Green Trees that in the Forest grew.

The Nymph complaining for the death
of her Faun

The wanton Troopers riding by
Have shot my Faun and it will dye.
Ungentle men! They cannot thrive
To kill thee. Thou neer didst alive
Them any harm: alas nor cou'd
Thy death yet do them any good.
I'me sure I never wisht them ill;
Nor do I for all this; nor will:
But, if my simple Pray'rs may yet
Prevail with Heaven to forget
Thy murder, I will Joyn my Tears
Rather then fail. But, O my fears!
It cannot dye so.* Heavens King
Keeps register of every thing:
And nothing may we use in vain.
Ev'n Beasts must be with justice slain;
Else Men are made their *Deodands*.*
Though they should wash their guilty hands
In this warm life-blood, which doth part
From thine, and wound me to the Heart,
Yet could they not be clean: their Stain
Is dy'd in such a Purple Grain.
There is not such another in
The World, to offer for their Sin.
   Unconstant *Sylvio*, when yet
I had not found him counterfeit,
One morning (I remember well)
Ty'd in this silver Chain and Bell,
Gave it to me: nay and I know
What he said then; I'me sure I do.

The Nymph complaining for the death of her Faun

Said He, look how your Huntsman here
Hath taught a Faun to hunt his *Dear*.
But *Sylvio* soon had me beguil'd.
This waxed tame, while he grew wild,
And quite regardless of my Smart,
Left me his Faun, but took his Heart.

   Thenceforth I set my self to play
My solitary time away,
With this: and very well content,
Could so mine idle Life have spent.
For it was full of sport; and light
Of foot, and heart; and did invite,
Me to its game: it seem'd to bless
Its self in me. How could I less
Than love it? O I cannot be
Unkind, t' a Beast that loveth me.

   Had it liv'd long, I do not know
Whether it too might have done so
As *Sylvio* did: his Gifts might be
Perhaps as false or more than he.
But I am sure, for ought that I
Could in so short a time espie,
Thy Love was far more better then
The love of false and cruel men.

   With sweetest milk, and sugar, first
I it at mine own fingers nurst.
And as it grew, so every day
It wax'd more white and sweet than they.
It had so sweet a Breath! And oft
I blusht to see its foot more soft,
And white, (shall I say then my hand?)
NAY any Ladies of the Land.

   It is a wond'rous thing, how fleet
'Twas on those little silver feet.

35

With what a pretty skipping grace,
It oft would challenge me the Race:
And when 'thad left me far away,
'Twould stay, and run again, and stay.
For it was nimbler much than Hindes;
And trod, as on the four Winds.
  I have a Garden of my own,
But so with Roses over grown,
And Lillies, that you would it guess
To be a little Wilderness.
And all the Spring time of the year
It onely loved to be there.
Among the bed of Lillies, I
Have sought it oft, where it should lye;
Yet could not, till it self would rise,
Find it, although before mine Eyes.
For, in the flaxen Lillies shade,
It like a bank of Lillies laid.
Upon the Roses it would feed,
Until its Lips ev'n seem'd to bleed:
And then to me 'twould boldly trip,
And print those Roses on my Lip.
But all its chief delight was still
On Roses thus its self to fill:
And its pure virgin Limbs to fold
In whitest sheets of Lillies cold.
Had it liv'd long, it would have been
Lillies without, Roses within.
  O help! O help! I see it faint:
And dye as calmely as a Saint.
See how it weeps. The Tears do come
Sad, slowly dropping like a Gumme.
So weeps the wounded Balsome: so
The holy Frankincense doth flow.

The Nymph complaining for the death of her Faun

The brotherless *Heliades*
Melt in such Amber Tears as these.
   I in a golden Vial will
Keep these two crystal Tears; and fill
It till it do o'reflow with mine;
Then place it in *Diana's* Shrine.
   Now my Sweet Faun is vanish'd to
Whether the Swans and Turtles go:
In fair *Elizium* to endure,
With milk-white Lambs, and Ermins pure.
O do not run too fast: for I
Will but bespeak thy Grave, and dye.
   First my unhappy Statue shall
Be cut in Marble; and withal,
Let it be weeping too: but there
Th' Engraver sure his Art may spare;
For I so truly thee bemoane,
That I shall weep though I be Stone:
Until my Tears, still dropping, wear
My breast, themselves engraving there.
There at my feet shalt thou be laid,
Of purest Alabaster made:
For I would have thine Image be
White as I can, though not as Thee.

Young Love

1

Come little Infant, Love me now,
  While thine unsuspected years
Clear thine aged Fathers brow
  From cold Jealousie and Fears.

2

Pretty surely 'twere to see
  By young Love old Time beguil'd:
While our Sportings are as free
  As the Nurses with the Child.

3

Common Beauties stay fifteen;
  Such as yours should swifter move;
Whose fair Blossoms are too green
  Yet for Lust, but not for Love.

4

Love as much the snowy Lamb
  Or the wanton Kid does prize,
As the lusty Bull or Ram,
  For his morning Sacrifice.

5

Now then love me: time may take
  Thee before thy time away:
Of this Need wee'l Virtue make,
  And learn Love before we may.

Young Love

6

So we win of doubtful Fate;
  And, if good she to us meant,
We that Good shall antedate,
  Or, if ill, that Ill prevent.

7

Thus as Kingdomes, frustrating
  Other Titles to their Crown,
In the craddle crown their King,
  So all Forraign Claims to drown,

8

So, to make all Rivals vain,
  Now I crown thee with my Love:
Crown me with thy Love again,
  And we both shall Monarchs prove.

To his Coy Mistress

Had we but World enough, and Time,
This coyness Lady were no crime.
We would sit down, and think which way
To walk, and pass our long Loves Day.
Thou by the *Indian Ganges* side
Should'st Rubies find: I by the Tide
Of *Humber* would complain. I would
Love you ten years before the Flood:
And you should if you please refuse
Till the Conversion of the *Jews*.
My vegetable Love should grow
Vaster then Empires, and more slow.
An hundred years should go to praise
Thine Eyes, and on thy Forehead Gaze.
Two hundred to adore each Breast:
But thirty thousand to the rest.
An Age at least to every part,
And the last Age should show your Heart.
For Lady you deserve this State;
Nor would I love at lower rate.
    But at my back I alwaies hear
Times winged Charriot hurrying near:
And yonder all before us lye
Desarts of vast Eternity.
Thy Beauty shall no more be found;
Nor, in thy marble Vault, shall sound
My ecchoing Song: then Worms shall try
That long preserv'd Virginity:
And your quaint Honour turn to dust;
And into ashes all my Lust.
The Grave's a fine and private place,

To his Coy Mistress

But none I think do there embrace.
  Now therefore, while the youthful hew
Sits on thy skin like morning dew,*
And while thy willing Soul transpires
At every pore with instant Fires,
Now let us sport us while we may;
And now, like am'rous birds of prey,
Rather at once our Time devour,
Than languish in his slow-chapt pow'r.*
Let us roll all our Strength, and all
Our sweetness, up into one Ball:
And tear our Pleasures with rough strife,
Thorough the Iron gates of Life.
Thus, though we cannot make our Sun
Stand still, yet we will make him run.

The unfortunate Lover

1

Alas, how pleasant are their dayes
With whom the Infant Love yet playes!
Sorted by pairs, they still are seen
By Fountains cool, and Shadows green.
But soon these Flames do lose their light,
Like Meteors of a Summers night:
Nor can they to that Region climb,
To make impression upon Time.

2

'Twas in a Shipwrack, when the Seas
Rul'd, and the Winds did what they please,
That my poor Lover floting lay,
And, e're brought forth, was cast away:
Till at the last the master-Wave
Upon the Rock his Mother drave;
And there she split against the Stone,
In a *Cesarian Section*.

3

The Sea him lent these bitter Tears
Which at his Eyes he alwaies bears.
And from the Winds the Sighs he bore,
Which through his surging Breast do roar.
No Day he saw but that which breaks,
Through frighted Clouds in forked streaks.
While round the ratling Thunder hurl'd,
As at the Fun'ral of the World.

The unfortunate Lover

4

While Nature to his Birth presents
This masque of quarrelling Elements;
A num'rous fleet of Corm'rants black,
That sail'd insulting o're the Wrack,
Receiv'd into their cruel Care,
Th' unfortunate and abject Heir:
Guardians most fit to entertain
The Orphan of the *Hurricane*.

5

They fed him up with Hopes and Air,
Which soon digested to Despair.
And as one Corm'rant fed him, still
Another on his Heart did bill.*
Thus while they famish him, and feast,
He both consumed, and increast:
And languished with doubtful Breath,
The' *Amphibium* of Life and Death.

6

And now, when angry Heaven wou'd
Behold a spectacle of Blood,
Fortune and He are call'd to play
At sharp* before it all the day:
And Tyrant Love his brest does ply
With all his wing'd Artillery.
Whilst he, betwixt the Flames and Waves,
Like *Ajax*, the mad Tempest braves.

7

See how he nak'd and fierce does stand,
Cuffing the Thunder with one hand;
While with the other he does lock,

And grapple, with the stubborn Rock:
From which he with each Wave rebounds,
Torn into Flames, and ragg'd with Wounds.
And all he saies, a Lover drest
In his own Blood does relish best.

8

This is the only *Banneret*★
That ever Love created yet:
Who though, by the Malignant Starrs,
Forced to live in Storms and Warrs:
Yet dying leaves a Perfume here,
And Musick within every Ear:
And he in Story only rules,
In a Field *Sable* a Lover *Gules*.

The Gallery

1

Clora come view my Soul, and tell
Whether I have contriv'd it well.
Now all its several lodgings lye
Compos'd into one Gallery;
And the great *Arras*-hangings, made
Of various Faces, by are laid;
That, for all furniture, you'l find
Only your Picture in my Mind.

2

Here Thou art painted in the Dress
Of an Inhumane Murtheress;
Examining* upon our Hearts
Thy fertile Shop of cruel Arts:
Engines more keen than ever yet
Adorned Tyrants Cabinet;
Of which the most tormenting are
Black Eyes, red Lips, and curled Hair.

3

But, on the other side, th' art drawn
Like to *Aurora* in the Dawn;
When in the East she slumb'ring lyes,
And stretches out her milky Thighs;
While all the morning Quire does sing,
And *Manna* falls, and Roses spring;
And, at thy Feet, the wooing Doves
Sit perfecting their harmless Loves.

The Gallery

4

Like an Enchantress here thou show'st,
Vexing thy restless Lover's Ghost;
And, by a Light obscure, dost rave
Over his Entrails, in the Cave;
Divining thence, with horrid Care,
How long thou shalt continue fair;
And (when inform'd) them throw'st away,
To be the greedy Vultur's prey.

5

But, against that, thou sit'st a float
Like *Venus* in her pearly Boat.
The *Halcyons*, calming all that's nigh,
Betwixt the Air and Water fly.
Or, if some rowling Wave appears,
A Mass of Ambergris it bears.
Nor blows more Wind than what may well
Convoy the Perfume to the Smell.

6

These Pictures and a thousand more,
Of Thee, my Gallery do store;
In all the Forms thou can'st invent
Either to please me, or torment:
For thou alone to people me,
Art grown a num'rous Colony;
And a Collection choicer far
Then or *White-hall's*, or *Mantua's* were.*

7

But, of these Pictures and the rest,
That at the Entrance likes me best:
Where the same Posture, and the Look

46

Remains, with which I first was took.
A tender Shepherdess, whose Hair
Hangs loosely playing in the Air,
Transplanting Flow'rs from the green Hill,
To crown her Head, and Bosome fill.

The Fair Singer

To make a final conquest of all me,
Love did compose so sweet an Enemy,
In whom both Beauties to my death agree,
Joyning themselves in fatal Harmony;
That while she with her Eyes my Heart does bind,
She with her Voice might captivate my Mind.

2

I could have fled from One but singly fair:
My dis-intangled Soul it self might save,
Breaking the curled trammels of her hair.
But how should I avoid to be her Slave,
Whose subtile Art invisibly can wreath
My Fetters of the very Air I breath?

3

It had been easie fighting in some plain,
Where Victory might hang in equal choice,
But all resistance against her is vain,
Who has th' advantage both of Eyes and Voice,
And all my Forces needs must be undone,
She having gained both the Wind and Sun.

Mourning

1

You, that decipher out the Fate
Of humane Off-springs from the Skies,
What mean these Infants which of late
Spring from the Starrs of *Chlora's* Eyes?

2

Her Eyes confus'd, and doubled ore,
With Tears suspended ere they flow;
Seem bending upwards, to restore
To Heaven, whence it came, their Woe.

3

When, molding* of the watry Sphears,
Slow drops unty themselves away;
As if she, with those precious Tears,
Would strow the ground where *Strephon* lay.

4

Yet some affirm, pretending Art,
Her Eyes have so her Bosome drown'd,
Only to soften near her Heart
A place to fix another Wound.

5

And, while vain Pomp does her restrain
Within her solitary Bowr,
She courts her self in am'rous Rain;
Her self both *Danae* and the Showr.

49

6

Nay others, bolder, hence esteem
Joy now so much her Master grown,
That whatsoever does but seem
Like Grief, is from her Windows thrown.

7

Nor that she payes, while she survives,
To her dead Love this Tribute due;
But casts abroad these Donatives,
At the installing of a new.

8

How wide they dream! The *Indian* Slaves
That sink for Pearl through Seas profound,
Would find her Tears yet deeper Waves
And not of one the bottom sound.

9

I yet my silent Judgment keep,
Disputing not what they believe
But sure as oft as Women weep,
It is to be suppos'd they grieve.

Daphnis and Chloe

1

Daphnis must from *Chloe* part:
Now is come the dismal Hour
That must all his Hopes devour,
All his Labour, all his Art.

2

Nature her own Sexes foe,
Long had taught her to be coy:
But she neither knew t'enjoy,
Nor yet let her Lover go.

3

But, with this sad News surpriz'd,
Soon she let that Niceness fall;
And would gladly yield to all,
So it had his stay compriz'd.*

4

Nature so her self does use
To lay by her wonted State,
Lest the World should separate;
Sudden Parting closer glews.

5

He, well read in all the wayes
By which men their Siege maintain,
Knew not that the Fort to gain
Better 'twas the Siege to raise.

6

But he came so full possest
With the Grief of Parting thence,
That he had not so much Sence
As to see he might be blest.

7

Till Love in her Language breath'd
Words she never spake before;
But then Legacies no more
To a dying Man bequeath'd.

8

For, Alas, the time was spent,
Now the latest minut's run
When poor *Daphnis* is undone,
Between Joy and Sorrow rent.

9

At that *Why*, that *Stay my Dear*,
His disorder'd Locks he tare;
And with rouling Eyes did glare,
And his cruel Fate forswear.

10

As the Soul of one scarce dead,
With the shrieks of Friends aghast,
Looks distracted back in hast,
And then streight again is fled.

11

So did wretched *Daphnis* look,
Frighting her he loved most.
At the last, this Lovers Ghost
Thus his Leave resolved took.

12

Are my Hell and Heaven Joyn'd
More to torture him that dies?
Could departure not suffice,
But that you must then grow kind?

13

Ah my *Chloe* how have I
Such a wretched minute found,
When thy Favours should me wound
More than all thy Cruelty?

14

So to the condemned Wight
The delicious Cup we fill;
And allow him all he will,
For his last and short Delight.

15

But I will not now begin
Such a Debt unto my Foe;
Nor to my Departure owe
What my Presence could not win.

16

Absence is too much alone:
Better 'tis to go in peace,
Than my Losses to increase
By a late Fruition.

17

Why should I enrich my Fate?
'Tis a Vanity to wear,
For my Executioner,
Jewels of so high a rate.

Daphnis and Chloe

18

Rather I away will pine
In a manly stubborness
Than be fatted up express
For the *Canibal* to dine.

19

Whilst this grief does thee disarm,
All th' Enjoyment of our Love
But the ravishment would prove
Of a Body dead while warm.

20

And I parting should appear
Like the Gourmand *Hebrew* dead,
While with Quailes and *Manna* fed,
He does through the Desert err.

21

Or the Witch that midnight wakes
For the Fern, whose magick Weed*
In one minute casts the Seed,
And invisible him makes.

22

Gentler times for Love are ment
Who for parting pleasure strain
Gather Roses in the rain,
Wet themselves and spoil their Sent.

23

Farewel therefore all the fruit
Which I could from Love receive:
Joy will not with Sorrow weave,
Nor will I this Grief pollute.

24

Fate I come, as dark, as sad,
As thy Malice could desire;
Yet bring with me all the Fire
That Love in his Torches had.

25

At these words away he broke;
As who long has praying ly'n,
To his Heads-man makes the Sign,
And receives the parting stroke.

26

But hence Virgins all beware.
Last night he with *Phlogis* slept;
This night for *Dorinda* kept;
And but rid to take the Air.

27

Yet he does himself excuse;
Nor indeed without a Cause.
For, according to the Lawes,
Why did *Chloe* once refuse?

The Definition of Love

I

My Love is of a birth as rare
As 'tis for object strange and high:
It was begotten by despair
Upon Impossibility.

2

Magnanimous Despair alone
Could show me so divine a thing,
Where feeble Hope could ne'r have flown
But vainly flapt its Tinsel Wing.

3

And yet I quickly might arrive
Where my extended Soul is fixt,
But Fate does Iron wedges drive,
And alwaies crouds it self betwixt.

4

For Fate with jealous Eye does see
Two perfect Loves; nor lets them close:
Their union would her ruine be,
And her Tyrannick pow'r depose.

5

And therefore her Decrees of Steel
Us as the distant Poles have plac'd,
(Though Loves whole World on us doth wheel)
Not by themselves to be embrac'd.

The Definition of Love

6

Unless the giddy Heaven fall,
And Earth some new Convulsion tear;
And, us to joyn, the World should all
Be cramp'd into a *Planisphere*.

7

As Lines so Loves *oblique* may well
Themselves in every Angle greet:
But ours so truly *Paralel*,
Though infinite can never meet.

8

Therefore the Love which us doth bind.
But Fate so enviously debarrs,
Is the Conjunction of the Mind,
And Opposition of the Stars.

The Picture of little T.C.* in a
Prospect of Flowers

1

See with what simplicity
This Nimph begins her golden daies!
In the green Grass she loves to lie,
And there with her fair Aspect tames
The Wilder flow'rs, and gives them names:
But only with the Roses playes;
          And them does tell
What Colour best becomes them, and what Smell.

2

Who can foretel for what high cause
This Darling of the Gods was born!
Yet this is She whose chaster Laws
The wanton Love shall one day fear,
And, under her command severe,
See his Bow broke and Ensigns torn.
          Happy, who can
Appease this virtuous Enemy of Man!

3

O then let me in time compound,
And parly with those conquering Eyes;
Ere they have try'd their force to wound,
Ere, with their glancing wheels, they drive
In Triumph over Hearts that strive,
And them that yield but* more despise.
          Let me be laid,
Where I may see thy Glories from some shade.

4

Mean time, whilst every verdant thing
It self does at thy Beauty charm,
Reform the errours of the Spring;
Make that the Tulips may have share
Of sweetness, seeing they are fair;
And Roses of their thorns disarm:
But most procure
That Violets may a longer Age endure.

5

But O young beauty of the Woods,
Whom Nature courts with fruits and flow'rs,
Gather the Flow'rs, but spare the Buds;
Lest *Flora* angry at thy crime,
To kill her Infants in their prime,
Do quickly make th' Example Yours;
And, ere we see,
Nip in the blossome all our hopes and Thee.

The Match

1

Nature had long a Treasure made
　　Of all her choisest store;
Fearing, when She should be decay'd,
　　To beg in vain for more.

2

Her *Orientest* Colours there,
　　And Essences most pure,
With sweetest Perfumes hoarded were,
　　All as she thought secure.

3

She seldom them unlock'd, or us'd,
　　But with the nicest care;
For, with one grain of them diffus'd,
　　She could the World repair.

4

But likeness soon together drew
　　What she did separate lay;
Of which one perfect Beauty grew,
　　And that was *Celia*.

5

Love wisely had for long fore-seen
　　That he must once grow old;
And therefore stor'd a Magazine,
　　To save him from the cold.

6

He kept the several Cells repleat
  With Nitre thrice refin'd;
The Naphta's and the Sulphurs heat,
  And all that burns the Mind.

7

He fortifi'd the double Gate,
  And rarely thither came;
For, with one Spark of these, he streight
  All Nature could inflame.

8

Till, by vicinity so long,
  A nearer Way they sought;
And, grown magnetically strong,
  Into each other wrought.

9

Thus all his fewel did unite
  To make one fire high:
None ever burn'd so hot, so bright;
  And *Celia* that am I.

10

So we alone the happy rest,
  Whilst all the World is poor,
And have within our Selves possest
  All Love's and Nature's store.

The Mower against Gardens

Luxurious* Man, to bring his Vice in use,
   Did after him the World seduce:
And from the fields the Flow'rs and Plants allure,
   Where Nature was most plain and pure.
He first enclos'd within the Gardens square
   A dead and standing pool of Air:
And a more luscious Earth for them did knead,
   Which stupifi'd them while it fed.
The Pink grew then as double as his Mind;
   The nutriment did change the kind.
With strange perfumes he did the Roses taint.
   And Flow'rs themselves were taught to paint.
The Tulip, white, did for complexion seek;
   And learn'd to interline its cheek:
Its Onion root* they then so high did hold,
   That one was for a Meadow sold.
Another World was search'd, through Oceans new,
   To find the *Marvel of Peru.**
And yet these Rarities might be allow'd,
   To Man, that sov'raign thing and proud;
Had he not dealt between the Bark and Tree,
   Forbidden mixtures there to see.
No Plant now knew the Stock from which it came;
   He grafts upon the Wild the Tame:
That the uncertain and adult'rate fruit
   Might put the Palate in dispute.
His green *Seraglio* has its Eunuchs too;
   Lest any Tyrant him out-doe.
And in the Cherry he does Nature vex,
   To procreate without a Sex.

The Mower against Gardens

'Tis all enforc'd; the Fountain and the Grot;
  While the sweet Fields do lye forgot:
Where willing Nature does to all dispence
  A wild and fragrant Innocence:
And *Fauns* and *Faryes* do the Meadows till,
  More by their presence then their skill.
Their Statues polish'd by some ancient hand,
  May to adorn the Gardens stand:
But howso'ere the Figures do excel,
  The *Gods* themselves with us do dwell.

Damon the Mower

1

Heark how the Mower *Damon* Sung,
With love of *Juliana*★ stung!
While ev'ry thing did seem to paint
The Scene more fit for his complaint.
Like her fair Eyes the day was fair;
But scorching like his am'rous Care.
Sharp like his Sythe his Sorrow was,
And wither'd like his Hopes the Grass.

2

Oh what unusual Heats are here,
Which thus our Sun-burn'd Meadows sear!
The Grass-hopper its pipe gives ore;
And hamstring'd★ Frogs can dance no more.
But in the brook the green Frog wades;
And Grass-hoppers seek out the shades.
Only the Snake, that kept within,
Now glitters in its second skin.

3

This heat the Sun could never raise,
Nor Dog-star so inflame's the dayes.
It from an higher Beauty grow'th,
Which burns the Fields and Mower both:
Which made the Dog, and makes the Sun
Hotter then his own *Phaeton*.
Not *July* causeth these Extremes,
But *Juliana's* scorching beams.

4

Tell me where I may pass the Fires
Of the hot day, or hot desires.
To what cool Cave shall I descend,
Or to what gelid Fountain bend?
Alas! I look for Ease in vain,
When Remedies themselves complain.
No moisture but my Tears do rest,
Nor Cold but in her Icy Breast.

5

How long wilt Thou, fair Shepheardess,
Esteem me, and my Presents less?
To Thee the harmless Snake I bring,
Disarmed of its teeth and sting.
To Thee *Chameleons* changing-hue,
And Oak leaves tipt with hony due.
Yet Thou ungrateful hast not sought
Nor what they are, nor who them brought.

6

I am the Mower *Damon*, known
Through all the Meadows I have mown.
On me the Morn her dew distills
Before her darling Daffadils.
And, if at Noon my toil me heat,
The Sun himself licks off my Sweat.
While, going home, the Ev'ning sweet
In cowslip-water bathes my feet.

7

What, though the piping Shepherd stock
The plains with an unnum'red Flock,
This Sithe of mine discovers wide

Damon the Mower

More ground then all his Sheep do hide.
With this the golden fleece I shear
Of all these Closes ev'ry Year.
And though in Wooll more poor then they,
Yet am I richer far in Hay.

8

Nor am I so deform'd to sight,
If in my Sithe I looked right;
In which I see my Picture done,
As in a crescent Moon the Sun.
The deathless Fairyes take me oft
To lead them in their Danses soft;
And, when I tune my self to sing,
About me they contract their Ring.

9

How happy might I still have mow'd,
Had not Love here his Thistles sow'd!
But now I all the day complain,
Joyning my Labour to my Pain;
And with my Sythe cut down the Grass,
Yet still my Grief is where it was:
But, when the Iron blunter grows,
Sighing I whet my Sythe and Woes.

10

While thus he threw his Elbow round,
Depopulating all the Ground,
And, with his whistling Sythe, does cut
Each stroke between the Earth and Root,
The edged Stele by careless chance
Did into his own Ankle glance;

66

And there among the Grass fell down,
By his own Sythe, the Mower mown.

II

Alas! said He, these hurts are slight
To those that dye by Loves despight.
With Shepherds-purse,* and Clowns-all-heal,*
The Blood I stanch, and Wound I seal.
Only for him no Cure is found,
Whom *Julianas* Eyes do wound.
'Tis death alone that this must do:
For Death thou art a Mower too.

The Mower to the Glo-Worms

1

Ye living Lamps, by whose dear light
The Nightingale does sit so late,
And studying all the Summer-night,
Her matchless Songs does meditate;

2

Ye Country Comets, that portend
No War, nor Princes funeral,
Shining unto no higher end
Then to presage the Grasses fall;

3

Ye Glo-worms, whose officious* Flame
To wandring Mowers shows the way,
That in the Night have lost their aim,
And after foolish Fires do stray;

4

Your courteous Lights in vain you wast,
Since *Juliana* here is come,
For She my Mind hath so displac'd
That I shall never find my home.

The Mower's Song

My Mind was once the true survey★
Of all these Medows fresh and gay;
And in the greenness of the Grass
Did see its Hopes as in a Glass;
When *Juliana* came, and She
What I do to the Grass, does to my Thoughts and Me.

2

But these, while I with Sorrow pine,
Grew more luxuriant still and fine;
That not one Blade of Grass you spy'd,
But had a Flower on either side;
When *Juliana* came, and She
What I do to the Grass, does to my Thoughts and Me.

3

Unthankful Medows, could you so
A fellowship so true forego,
And in your gawdy May-games meet,
While I lay trodden under feet?
When *Juliana* came, and She
What I do to the Grass, does to my Thoughts and Me.

4

But what you in Compassion ought,
Shall now by my Revenge be wrought:
And Flow'rs, and Grass, and I and all,
Will in one common Ruine fall.
For *Juliana* comes, and She
What I do to the Grass, does to my Thoughts and Me.

The Mower's Song

And thus, ye Meadows, which have been
Companions of my thoughts more green,
Shall now the Heraldry become
With which I shall adorn my Tomb;
For *Juliana* comes, and She
What I do to the Grass, does to my Thoughts and Me.

Ametas and Thestylis making Hay-Ropes

1
Ametas

Think'st Thou that this Love can stand,
Whilst Thou still dost say me nay?
Love unpaid does soon disband:
Love binds Love as Hay binds Hay.

2
Thestylis

Think'st Thou that this Rope would twine
If we both should turn one way?
Where both parties so combine,
Neither Love will twist nor Hay.

3
Ametas

Thus you vain Excuses find,
Which your selve and us delay:
And Love tyes a Womans Mind
Looser then with Ropes of Hay.

4
Thestylis

What you cannot constant hope
Must be taken as you may.

5
Ametas

Then let's both lay by our Rope,
And go kiss within the Hay.

Musicks Empire

1

First was the World as one great Cymbal made,
Where Jarring Windes to infant Nature plaid.
All Musick was a solitary sound,
To hollow Rocks and murm'ring Fountains bound.

2

Jubal first made the wilder Notes agree;
And *Jubal* tuned Musicks *Jubilee*:
He call'd the *Ecchoes* from their sullen Cell,
And built the Organs City where they dwell.

3

Each sought a consort in that lovely place;
And Virgin Trebles wed the manly Base.
From whence the Progeny of numbers new
Into harmonious Colonies withdrew.

4

Some to the Lute, some to the Viol went,
And others chose the Cornet eloquent.
These practising the Wind, and those the Wire,
To sing Mens Triumphs, or in Heavens quire.

5

Then Musick, the Mosaique of the Air,
Did of all these a solemn noise prepare:
With which She gain'd the Empire of the Ear,
Including all between the Earth and Sphear.

Musicks Empire

6

Victorious sounds! yet here your Homage do
Unto a gentler Conqueror then you;
Who though He flies the Musick of his praise,
Would with you Heavens Hallelujahs raise.

The Garden

1

How vainly men themselves amaze
To win the Palm, the Oke, or Bayes;*
And their uncessant Labours see
Crown'd from some single Herb or Tree.
Whose short and narrow verged Shade
Does prudently their Toyles upbraid;
While all Flow'rs and all Trees do close
To weave the Garlands of repose.

2

Fair quiet, have I found thee here,
And Innocence thy Sister dear!
Mistaken long, I sought you then
In busie Companies of Men.
Your sacred Plants, if here below,
Only among the Plants will grow.
Society is all but* rude,
To this delicious Solitude.

3

No white nor red was ever seen
So am'rous as this lovely green.
Fond Lovers, cruel as their Flame,
Cut in these Trees their Mistress name.
Little, Alas, they know, or heed,
How far these Beauties Hers exceed!
Fair Trees! where s'eer your barkes I wound,
No Name shall but your own be found.

74

4

When we have run our Passions heat,
Love hither makes his best retreat.
The *Gods*, that mortal Beauty chase,
Still in a Tree did end their race.
Apollo hunted *Daphne* so,
Only that She might Laurel grow.
And *Pan* did after *Syrinx* speed,
Not as a Nymph, but for a Reed.

5

What wond'rous Life in this I lead!
Ripe Apples drop about my head;
The Luscious Clusters of the Vine
Upon my Mouth do crush their Wine;
The Nectaren, and curious* Peach,
Into my hands themselves do reach;
Stumbling on Melons, as I pass,
Insnar'd with Flow'rs, I fall on Grass.

6

Mean while the Mind, from pleasure less,
Withdraws into its happiness:
The Mind, that Ocean where each kind
Does streight its own resemblance find;
Yet it creates, transcending these,
Far other Worlds, and other Seas;
Annihilating all that's made
To a green Thought* in a green Shade.

7

Here at the Fountains sliding foot,
Or at some Fruit-trees mossy root,
Casting the Bodies Vest aside,

The Garden

My Soul into the boughs does glide:
There like a Bird it sits, and sings,
Then whets,* and combs its silver Wings;
And, till prepar'd for longer flight,
Waves in its Plumes the various Light.

8

Such was that happy Garden-state,
While Man there walk'd without a Mate:
After a Place so pure, and sweet,
What other Help could yet be meet!
But 'twas beyond a Mortal's share
To wander solitary there:
Two Paradises 'twere in one
To live in Paradise alone.

9

How well the skilful Gardner drew
Of flow'rs and herbes this Dial new;
Where from above the milder Sun
Does through a fragrant Zodiack run;
And, as it works, th' industrious Bee
Computes its time as well as we.
How could such sweet and wholsome Hours
Be reckon'd but with herbs and flow'rs!

An Epitaph upon ——

Enough: and leave the rest to Fame.
'Tis to commend her but to name.
Courtship, which living she declin'd,
When dead to offer were unkind.
Where never any could speak ill,
Who would officious Praises spill?
Nor can the truest Wit or Friend,
Without Detracting, her commend.
To say she liv'd a *Virgin* chast,
In this Age loose and all unlac't;
Nor was, when Vice is so allow'd,
Of *Virtue* or asham'd, or proud;
That her Soul was on *Heaven* so bent
No Minute but it came and went;
That ready her last Debt to pay
She summ'd her Life up ev'ry day;
Modest as Morn; as Mid-day bright;
Gentle as Ev'ning; cool as Night;
'Tis true: but all so weakly said;
'Twere more Significant, *She's Dead.*

Upon the Hill and Grove at Bill-borow
To the Lord Fairfax

1

See how the arched Earth does here
Rise in a perfect Hemisphere!
The stiffest Compass could not strike
A Line more circular and like;
Nor softest Pensel draw a Brow
So equal as this Hill does bow.
It seems as for a Model laid,
And that the World by it was made.

2

Here learn ye Mountains more unjust,
Which to abrupter greatness thrust,
That do with your hook-shoulder'd height
The Earth deform and Heaven fright,
For* whose excrescence ill design'd,
Nature must a new Center find,
Learn here those humble steps to tread,
Which to securer Glory lead.

3

See what a soft access and wide
Lyes open to its grassy side;
Nor with the rugged path deterrs
The feet of breathless Travellers.
See then how courteous it ascends,
And all the way it rises bends;
Nor for it self the height does gain,
But only strives to raise the Plain.

4

Yet thus it all the field commands,
And in unenvy'd Greatness stands,
Discerning further then the Cliff
Of Heaven-daring *Teneriff*.
How glad the weary Seamen hast
When they salute it from the Mast!
By Night the Northern Star their way
Directs, and this no less by Day.

5

Upon its crest this Mountain grave
A Plump of aged Trees does wave.
No hostile hand durst ere invade
With impious Steel the sacred Shade.
For something alwaies did appear
Of the *great Masters* terrour there:
And Men could hear his Armour still
Ratling through all the Grove and Hill.

6

Fear of the *Master*, and respect
Of the great *Nymph* did it protect;
Vera★ the *Nymph* that him inspir'd,
To whom he often here retir'd,
And on these Okes ingrav'd her Name;
Such Wounds alone these Woods became:
But ere he well the Barks could part
'Twas writ already in their Heart.

7

For they ('tis credible) have sense,
As We, of Love and Reverence,
And underneath the Courser Rind

79

The *Genius* of the house do bind.
Hence they successes seem to know,
And in their *Lord's* advancement grow;
But in no Memory were seen
As under this* so streight and green.

8

Yet now no further strive to shoot,
Contented if they fix their Root.
Nor to the winds uncertain gust,
Their prudent Heads too far intrust.
Onely sometimes a flutt'ring Breez
Discourses with the breathing Trees;
Which in their modest Whispers name
Those Acts that swell'd the Cheek of Fame.

9

Much other Groves, say they, then these
And other Hills him once did please.
Through Groves of Pikes he thunder'd then,
And Mountains rais'd of dying Men.
For all the *Civick Garlands* due
To him our Branches are but few.
Nor are our Trunks enow to bear
The *Trophees* of one fertile Year.

10

'Tis true, ye Trees nor ever spoke
More certain *Oracles* in Oak.*
But Peace (if you his favour prize)
That Courage its own Praises flies.
Therefore to your obscurer Seats
From his own Brightness he retreats:
Nor he the Hills without the Groves,
Nor Height but with Retirement loves.

Upon Appleton House, to my Lord Fairfax*

1

Within this sober Frame expect
Work of no Forrain *Architect*;
That unto Caves the Quarries drew,
And Forrests did to Pastures hew;
Who of his great Design in pain
Did for a Model vault* his Brain,
Whose Columnes should so high be rais'd
To arch the Brows that on them gaz'd.

2

Why should of all things Man unrul'd
Such unproportion'd dwellings built?
The Beasts are by their Denns exprest:
And Birds contrive an equal Nest;
The low roof'd Tortoises do dwell
In cases fit of Tortoise-shell:
No Creature loves an empty space;
Their Bodies measure out their Place.

3

But He, superfluously spread,
Demands more room alive then dead.
And in his hollow Palace goes
Where Winds as he themselves may lose.
What need of all this Marble Crust
T'impark the wanton Mote of Dust,
That thinks by Breadth the World t'unite
Though the first Builders fail'd in Height?

4

But all things are composed here
Like Nature, orderly and near:
In which we the Dimensions find
Of that more sober Age and Mind,
When larger sized Men did stoop
To enter at a narrow loop;*
As practising, in doors so strait,
To strain themselves through *Heavens Gate*.

5

And surely when the after Age
Shall hither come in *Pilgrimage*,
These sacred Places to adore,
By *Vere** and *Fairfax* trod before,
Men will dispute how their Extent
Within such dwarfish Confines went:
And some will smile at this, as well
As *Romulus* his Bee-like Cell.*

6

Humility alone designs
Those short but admirable Lines,
By which, ungirt and unconstrain'd,
Things greater are in less contain'd.
Let others vainly strive t'immure
The *Circle* in the *Quadrature*!
These *holy Mathematicks* can
In ev'ry Figure equal Man.

7

Yet thus the laden House does sweat,
And scarce indures the *Master* great:
But where he comes the swelling Hall

Stirs, and the *Square* grows *Spherical*,★
More by his *Magnitude* distrest,
Then he is by its straitness prest:
And too officiously it slights
That in it self which him delights.

8

So Honour better Lowness bears,
Then That unwonted Greatness wears.
Height with a certain Grace does bend,
But low Things clownishly ascend.
And yet what needs there here Excuse,
Where ev'ry Thing does answer Use?
Where neatness nothing can condemn,
Nor Pride invent what to contemn?

9

A Stately *Frontispice*★ of *Poor*
Adorns without the open Door:
Nor less the Rooms within commends
Daily new *Furniture of Friends*.
The House was built upon the Place
Only as for *a Mark of Grace*;★
And for an *Inn* to entertain
Its *Lord* a while, but not remain.

10

Him *Bishops-Hill*, or *Denton* may,★
Or *Bilbrough*, better hold then they:
But Nature here hath been so free
As if she said leave this to me.
Art would more neatly have defac'd
What she had laid so sweetly wast;
In fragrant Gardens, shaddy Woods,
Deep Meadows, and transparent Floods.

11

While with slow Eyes we these survey,
And on each pleasant footstep stay,
We opportunly may relate
The Progress of this Houses Fate.*
A *Nunnery* first gave it birth.
For *Virgin Buildings* oft brought forth.
And all that Neighbour-Ruine shows
The Quarries whence this dwelling rose.

12

Near to this gloomy Cloysters Gates
There dwelt the blooming Virgin *Thwates*;
Fair beyond Measure, and an Heir
Which might Deformity make fair.
And oft She spent the Summer Suns
Discoursing with the *Suttle Nunns*.
Whence in these Words one to her weav'd,
(As 'twere by Chance) Thoughts long conceiv'd.

13

'Within this holy leisure we
'Live innocently as you see.
'These Walls restrain the World without,
'But hedge our Liberty about.
'These Bars inclose that wider Den
'Of those wild Creatures, called Men.
'The Cloyster outward shuts its Gates,
'And, from us, locks on them the Grates.

14

'Here we, in shining Armour white,*
'Like *Virgin Amazons* do fight.
'And our chast *Lamps* we hourly trim,

'Lest the great *Bridegroom* find them dim.
'Our *Orient* Breaths perfumed are
'With insense of incessant Pray'r.
'And Holy-water of our Tears
'Most strangly our Complexion clears.

15

'Not Tears of Grief; but such as those
'With which calm Pleasure overflows;
'Or Pity, when we look on you
'That live without this happy Vow.
'How should we grieve that must be seen
'Each one a *Spouse*, and each a *Queen*;
'And can in *Heaven* hence behold
'Our brighter Robes and Crowns of Gold?

16

'When we have prayed all our Beads,
'Some One the holy *Legend* reads;
'While all the rest with Needles paint
'The Face and Graces of the *Saint*.
'But what the Linnen can't receive
'They in their Lives do interweave.
'This Work the *Saints* best represents;
'That serves for *Altar's Ornaments*.

17

'But much it to our work would add
'If here your hand, your Face we had:
'By it we would *our Lady* touch;
'Yet thus* She you resembles much.
'Some of your Features, as we sow'd,
'Through ev'ry *Shrine* should be bestow'd.
'And in one Beauty we would take
'Enough a thousand *Saints* to make.

85

18

'And (for I dare not quench the Fire
'That me does for your good inspire)
''Twere Sacriledge a Man t'admit
'To holy things, for *Heaven* fit.
'I see the *Angels* in a Crown
'On you the Lillies show'ring down:
'And round about you Glory breaks,
'That something more then humane speaks.

19

'All Beauty, when at such a height,
'Is so already consecrate.
'*Fairfax* I know; and long ere this
'Have mark'd the Youth, and what he is.
'But can he such a *Rival* seem
'For whom you *Heav'n* should disesteem?
'Ah, no! and 'twould more Honour prove
'He your *Devoto* were, then *Love*.

20

'Here live beloved, and obey'd:
'Each one your Sister, each your Maid.
'And, if our Rule seem strictly pend,
'The Rule it self to you shall bend.
'Our *Abbess* too, now far in Age,
'Doth your succession near presage.
'How soft the yoke on us would lye,
'Might such fair Hands as yours it tye!

21

'Your voice, the sweetest of the Quire,
'Shall draw *Heav'n* nearer, raise us higher.
'And your Example, if our Head,

86

'Will soon us to perfection lead.
'Those Virtues to us all so dear,
'Will straight grow Sanctity when here:
'And that, once sprung, increase so fast
'Till Miracles it work at last.

22

'Nor is our *Order* yet so nice,
'Delight to banish as a Vice.
'Here Pleasure Piety doth meet;
'One perfecting the other Sweet.
'So through the mortal fruit we boyl
'The Sugars uncorrupting Oyl:
'And that which perisht while we pull,
'Is thus preserved clear and full.

23

'For such indeed are all our Arts;
'Still handling Natures finest Parts.
'Flow'rs dress the Altars; for the Clothes,
'The Sea-born Amber we compose;*
'Balms for the griv'd* we draw; and Pasts
'We mold, as Baits for curious tasts.
'What need is here of Man? unless
'These as sweet Sins we should confess.

24

'Each Night among us to your side
'Appoint a fresh and Virgin Bride;
'Whom if *our Lord* at midnight find,
'Yet Neither should be left behind.
'Where you may lye as chast in Bed,
'As Pearls together billeted.
'All Night embracing Arm in Arm,
'Like Chrystal pure with Cotton warm.

25

'But what is this to all the store
'Of Joys you see, and may make more!
'Try but a while, if you be wise:
'The Tryal neither Costs, nor Tyes.
Now *Fairfax* seek her promis'd faith:
Religion that dispensed hath;
Which She hence forward does begin:*
The *Nuns* smooth Tongue has suckt her in.

26

Oft, though he knew it was in vain,
Yet would he valiantly complain.
'Is this that *Sanctity* so great,
'An Art by which you finly'r cheat?
'Hypocrite Witches, hence *avant*,
'Who though in prison yet inchant!
'Death only can such Theeves make fast,
'As rob though in the Dungeon cast.

27

'Were there but, when this House was made,
'One Stone that a just Hand had laid,
'It must have fall'n upon her Head
'Who first Thee from thy Faith misled.
'And yet, how well soever ment,
'With them 'twould soon grow fraudulent:
'For like themselves they alter all,
'And vice infects the very Wall.

28

'But sure those Buildings last not long,
'Founded by Folly, kept by Wrong.
'I know what Fruit their Gardens yield,

'When they it think by Night conceal'd.
'Fly from their Vices. 'Tis thy state,*
'Not Thee, that they would consecrate.
'Fly from their Ruine. How I fear
'Though guiltless lest thou perish there.

29

What should he do? He would respect
Religion, but not Right neglect:
For first Religion taught him Right,
And dazled not but clear'd his sight.
Sometimes resolv'd his Sword he draws,
But reverenceth then the Laws:
For Justice still that Courage led;
First from a Judge, then Souldier* bred.

30

Small Honour would be in the Storm.
The *Court* him grants the lawful Form;
Which licens'd either Peace or Force,
To hinder the unjust Divorce.
Yet still the *Nuns* his Right debar'd,
Standing upon their holy Guard.
Ill-counsell'd Women, do you know
Whom you resist, or what you do?

31

Is not this he whose Offspring fierce
Shall fight through all the *Universe*;
And with successive Valour try
France, Poland, either *Germany*;*
Till one, as long since prophecy'd,
His Horse through conquer'd *Britain* ride?
Yet, against Fate, his Spouse they kept;
And the great Race would intercept.

32

Some to the Breach against their Foes
Their *Wooden Saints* in vain oppose.
Another bolder stands at push
With their old *Holy-Water Brush*.
While the disjointed★ *Abbess* threads
The gingling Chain-shot of her *Beads*.
But their lowd'st Cannon were their Lungs;
And sharpest Weapons were their Tongues.

33

But, waving these aside like Flyes,
Young *Fairfax* through the Wall does rise.
Then th' unfrequented Vault appear'd,
And superstitions vainly fear'd.
The *Relicks false* were set to view;
Only the Jewels there were true.
But truly bright and holy *Thwaites*
That weeping at the *Altar* waites.

34

But the glad Youth away her bears,
And to the *Nuns* bequeaths her Tears:
Who guiltily their Prize bemoan,
Like Gipsies that a Child hath stoln.
Thenceforth (as when th'Inchantment ends
The Castle vanishes or rends)
The wasting Cloister with the rest
Was in one instant dispossest.

35

At the demolishing, this Seat
To *Fairfax* fell as by Escheat.
And what both *Nuns* and *Founders* will'd

'Tis likely better thus fulfill'd.
For if the *Virgin* prov'd not theirs,
The *Cloyster* yet remained hers.
Though many a *Nun* there made her Vow,
'Twas no *Religious House* till now.

36

From that blest Bed the *Heroe* came,
Whom *France* and *Poland* yet does fame:
Who, when retired here to Peace,
His warlike Studies could not cease;
But laid these Gardens out in sport
In the just Figure of a Fort;
And with five Bastions it did fence,
As aiming one for ev'ry Sense.★

37

When in the *East* the Morning Ray
Hangs out the Colours of the Day,
The Bee through these known Allies hums,
Beating the *Dian* with its *Drumms*.
Then Flow'rs their drowsie Eylids raise,
Their Silken Ensigns each displayes,
And dries its Pan★ yet dank with Dew,
And fills its Flask★ with Odours new.

38

These, as their *Governour* goes by,
In fragrant Vollyes they let fly;
And to salute their *Governess*
Again as great a charge they press:
None for the *Virgin Nymph*; for She
Seems with the Flow'rs a Flow'r to be.
And think so still! though not compare★
With Breath so sweet, or Cheek so faire.

39

Well shot ye Firemen! Oh how sweet,
And round your equal Fires do meet;
Whose shrill report no Ear can tell,
But Ecchoes to the Eye and smell.
See how the Flow'rs, as at *Parade*,
Under their *Colours* stand displaid:
Each *Regiment* in order grows,
That of the Tulip Pinke and Rose.

40

But when the vigilant *Patroul*
Of Stars walks round about the *Pole*,
Their Leaves, that to the stalks are curl'd,
Seem to their Staves the *Ensigns* furl'd.
Then in some Flow'rs beloved Hut
Each Bee as Sentinel is shut;
And sleeps so too: but, if once stir'd,
She runs you through, or askes *the Word*.

41

Oh Thou, that dear and happy Isle
The Garden of the World ere while,
Thou *Paradise* of four Seas,
Which *Heaven* planted us to please,
But, to exclude the World, did guard
With watry if not flaming Sword;
What luckless Apple did we tast,
To make us Mortal, and The Wast?

42

Unhappy! shall we never more
That sweet *Militia* restore,
When Gardens only had their Towrs,

And all the Garrisons were Flowrs,
When Roses only Arms might bear,
And Men did rosie Garlands wear?
Tulips, in several Colours barr'd,
Were then the *Switzers* of our *Guard*.★

43

The *Gardiner* had the *Souldiers* place,
And his more gentle Forts did trace.
The Nursery of all things green
Was then the only *Magazeen*.
The *Winter Quarters* were the Stoves,
Where he the tender Plants removes.
But War all this doth overgrow:
We Ord'nance Plant and Powder sow.

44

And yet their walks one on the Sod
Who, had it pleased him and *God*,
Might once have made our Gardens spring
Fresh as his own and flourishing.
But he preferr'd to the *Cinque Ports*★
These five imaginary Forts:
And, in those half-dry Trenches, spann'd★
Pow'r which the Ocean might command.

45

For he did, with his utmost Skill,
Ambition weed, but *Conscience* till.
Conscience, that Heaven-nursed Plant,
Which most our Earthly Gardens want.
A prickling leaf it bears, and such
As that which shrinks at ev'ry touch,★
But Flowrs eternal, and divine,
That in the Crowns of Saints do shine.

46

The sight does from these *Bastions* ply,
Th' invisible *Artilery*;
And at proud *Cawood Castle*★ seems
To point the *Battery* of its Beams.
As if it quarrell'd★ in the Seat
Th' Ambition of its *Prelate* great.
But ore the Meads below it plays,
Or innocently seems to gaze.

47

And now to the Abbyss I pass
Of that unfathomable Grass,
Where Men like Grashoppers appear,
But Grashoppers are Gyants there:
They, in there squeking Laugh, contemn
Us as we walk more low then them:
And, from the Precipices tall
Of the green spir's, to us do call.

48

To see Men through this Meadow Dive,
We wonder how they rise alive.
As, under Water, none does know
Whether he fall through it or go.★
But, as the Marriners that sound,
And show upon their Lead the Ground,
They bring up Flow'rs so to be seen,
And prove they've at the Bottom been.

49

No Scene★ that turns with Engines strange
Does oftner then these Meadows change.
For when the Sun the Grass hath vext,

The tawny Mowers enter next;
Who seem like *Israalites* to be,
Walking on foot through a green *Sea*.
To them the Grassy Deeps divide,
And crowd a Lane to either Side.*

50

With whistling Sithe, and Elbow strong,
These Massacre the Grass along:
While one, unknowing, carves the *Rail*,*
Whose yet unfeather'd Quils her fail.
The Edge all bloody from its Breast
He draws, and does his stroke detest;
Fearing the Flesh untimely mow'd
To him a Fate as black forebode.

51

But bloody *Thestylis*, that waites
To bring the mowing Camp their Cates,
Greedy as Kites has trust it up,
And forthwith means on it to sup:
When on another quick She lights,
And cryes, he call'd us *Israelites*;
But now, to make his saying true,
Rails rain for Quails, for Manna Dew.

52

Unhappy Birds! what does it boot
To build below the Grasses Root;
When Lowness is unsafe as Hight,
And Chance o'retakes what scapeth spight?
And now your Orphan Parents Call
Sounds your untimely Funeral.
Death-Trumpets creak in such a Note,
And 'tis the *Sourdine** in their Throat.

53

Or sooner hatch or higher build:
The Mower now commands the Field;
In whose new Traverse seemeth wrought
A Camp of Battail newly fought:
Where, as the Meads with Hay, the Plain
Lyes quilted ore with Bodies slain:
The Women that with forks it fling,
Do represent the Pillaging.

54

And now the careless Victors play,
Dancing the Triumphs of the Hay;★
Where every Mowers wholesome Heat
Smells like an *Alexanders sweat*.★
Their Females fragrant as the Mead
Which they in *Fairy Circles* tread:
When at their Dances End they kiss,
Their new-made Hay not sweeter is.

55

When after this 'tis pil'd in Cocks,
Like a calm Sea it shews the Rocks;
We wondring in the River near
How Boats among them safely steer.
Or, like the *Desert Memphis Sand*,
Short *Pyramids* of Hay do stand.
And such the *Roman Camps* do rise
In Hills for Soldiers Obsequies.

56

This *Scene* again withdrawing brings
A new and empty Face of things;
A levell'd space, as smooth and plain,

As Clothes for *Lilly*★ strecht to stain.
The World when first created sure
Was such a Table rase and pure.
Or rather such is the *Toril*★
Ere the Bulls enter at Madril.★

57

For to this naked equal Flat,
Which *Levellers* take Pattern at,
The Villagers in common chase
Their Cattle, which it closer rase;
And what below the Sith increast
Is pincht yet nearer by the Beast.
Such, in the painted World, appear'd
Davenant with th' Universal Heard.

58

They seem within the polisht Grass
A Landskip drawen in Looking-Glass.★
And shrunk in the huge Pasture show
As Spots, so shap'd, on Faces do.
Such Fleas, ere they approach the Eye,
In Multiplying Glasses lye.★
They feed so wide, so slowly move,
As *Constellations* do above.

59

Then, to conclude these pleasant Acts,
Denton sets ope its *Cataracts*;
And makes the Meadow truly be
(What it but seem'd before) a Sea.
For, jealous of its *Lords* long stay,
It try's t'invite him thus away.
The River in it self is drown'd,
And Isl's th' astonish'd Cattle round.

60

Let others tell the *Paradox*,
How Eels now bellow in the Ox;
How Horses at their Tails do kick,
Turn'd as they hang to Leeches quick;★
How Boats can over Bridges sail;
And Fishes do the Stables scale.
How *Salmons* trespassing are found;
And Pikes are taken in the Pound.

61

But I, retiring from the Flood,
Take Sanctuary in the Wood;
And, while it lasts, my self imbark
In this yet green, yet growing Ark;
Where the first Carpenter might best
Fit Timber for his Keel have Prest.
And where all Creatures might have shares,
Although in Armies, not in Paires.

62

The double Wood of ancient Stocks
Link'd in so thick, an Union locks,★
It like two *Pedigrees* appears,
On one hand *Fairfax*, th' other *Veres*:
Of whom though many fell in War,★
Yet more to Heaven shooting are:
And, as they Natures Cradle deckt,
Will in green Age her Hearse expect.

63

When first the Eye this Forrest sees
It seems indeed as *Wood* not *Trees*:
As if their Neighbourhood★ so old

To one great Trunk them all did mold.
There the huge Bulk takes place, as ment
To thrust up a *Fifth Element*;
And stretches still so closely wedg'd
As if the Night within were hedg'd.

64

Dark all without it knits; within
It opens passable and thin;
And in as loose an order grows,
As the *Corinthean Porticoes*.
The arching Boughs unite between
The Columnes of the Temple green;
And underneath the winged Quires
Echo about their tuned Fires.

65

The *Nightingale* does here make choice
To sing the Tryals of her Voice.
Low Shrubs she sits in, and adorns
With Musick high the squatted Thorns.
But highest Oakes stoop down to hear,
And listning Elders prick the Ear.
The Thorn, lest it should hurt her, draws
Within the Skin its shrunken claws.

66

But I have for my Musick found
A Sadder, yet more pleasing Sound:
The *Stock-doves*, whose fair necks are grac'd
With Nuptial Rings their Ensigns chast;
Yet always, for some Cause unknown,
Sad pair unto the Elms they moan.
O why should such a Couple mourn,
That in so equal Flames do burn!

67

Then as I carless on the Bed
Of gelid *Straw-berryes* do tread,
And through the Hazles thick espy
The hatching *Thrastles* shining Eye,
The *Heron* from the Ashes top,
The eldest of its young lets drop,
As if it Stork-like★ did pretend
That *Tribute* to *its Lord* to send.

68

But most the *Hewel's*★ wonders are,
Who here has the *Holt-felsters*★ care.
He walks still upright from the Root,
Meas'ring the Timber with his Foot;
And all the way, to keep it clean,
Doth from the Bark the Wood-moths glean.
He, with his Beak, examines well
Which fit to stand and which to fell.

69

The good he numbers up, and hacks;
As if he mark'd them with the Ax.
But where he, tinkling with his Beak,
Does find the hollow Oak to speak,
That for his building he designs,
And through the tainted Side he mines.
Who could have thought the *tallest Oak*
Should fall by such a *feeble Strok'*!

70

Nor would it, had the Tree not fed
A *Traitor-worm*, within it bred.
(As first our *Flesh* corrupt within

Tempts impotent and bashful *Sin*.)
And yet that *Worm* triumphs not long,
But serves to feed the *Hewels young*.
While the Oake seems to fall content,
Viewing the Treason's Punishment.

71

Thus I, *easie Philosopher*,
Among the *Birds* and *Trees* confer:
And little now to make me, wants
Or of the *Fowles*, or of the *Plants*.
Give me but Wings as they, and I
Streight floting on the Air shall fly:
Or turn me but, and you shall see
I was but an inverted *Tree*.

72

Already I begin to call
In their most learned Original:
And where I Language want, my Signs
The Bird upon the Bough divines;
And more attentive there doth sit
Then if She were with Lime-twigs knit.
No Leaf does tremble in the Wind
Which I returning cannot find.

73

Out of these scatter'd *Sibyls* Leaves
Strange *Prophecies* my Phancy weaves:
And in one History consumes,
Like *Mexique Paintings*, all the *Plumes*.
What *Rome*, *Greece*, *Palestine*, ere said
I in this light *Mosaick* read.
Thrice happy he who, not mistook,
Hath read in *Natures mystick Book*.

74

And see how Chance's better Wit
Could with a Mask my studies hit!*
The Oak-Leaves me embroyder all,
Between which Caterpillars crawl:
And Ivy, with familiar trails,
Me licks, and clasps, and curles, and hales.
Under this *antick Cope* I move
Like some great *Prelate of the Grove.*

75

Then, languishing with ease, I toss
On Pallets swoln of Velvet Moss;
While the Wind, cooling through the Boughs,
Flatters with Air my panting Brows.
Thanks for my Rest ye *Mossy Banks*,
And unto you *cool Zephyr's* Thanks,
Who, as my Hair, my Thoughts too shed,*
And winnow from the Chaff my Head.

76

How safe, methinks, and strong, behind
These Trees have I incamp'd my Mind;
Where Beauty, aiming at the Heart,
Bends in some Tree its useless Dart;
And where the World no certain Shot
Can make, or me it toucheth not.
But I on it securely play,
And gaul its Horsemen all the Day.

77

Bind me ye *Woodbines* in your 'twines,
Curle me about ye gadding *Vines*,
And Oh so close your Circles lace,

That I may never leave this Place:
But, lest your Fetters prove too weak,
Ere I your Silken Bondage break,
Do you, *O Brambles*, chain me too,
And courteous *Briars* nail me through.

78

Here in the Morning tye my Chain,
Where the two Woods have made a Lane;
While, like a *Guard* on either side,
The Trees before their *Lord* divide;
This, like a long and equal Thread,
Betwixt two *Labyrinths* does lead.
But, where the Floods did lately drown,
There at the Ev'ning stake me down.

79

For now the Waves are fal'n and dry'd,
And now the Meadows fresher dy'd;
Whose Grass, with moister colour dasht,
Seems as green Silks but newly washt.
No *Serpent* new nor *Crocodile*
Remains behind our little *Nile*;
Unless it self you will mistake,
Among these Meads the only Snake.

80

See in what wanton harmless folds
It ev'ry where the Meadow holds;
And its yet muddy back doth lick,
Till as a *Chrystal Mirrour* slick;*
Where all things gaze themselves, and doubt
If they be in it or without.
And for his shade which therein shines,
Narcissus like, the *Sun* too pines.

81

Oh what a Pleasure 'tis to hedge
My Temples here with heavy sedge;
Abandoning my lazy Side,
Stretcht as a Bank unto the Tide;
Or to suspend my sliding Foot
On the Osiers undermined Root,
And in its Branches tough to hang,
While at my Lines the Fishes twang!

82

But now away my Hooks, my Quills,*
And Angles, idle Utensils.
The *young Maria* walks to night:
Hide trifling Youth thy Pleasures slight.
'Twere shame that such judicious Eyes
Should with such Toys a Man surprize;
She that already is the *Law*
Of all her *Sex*, her *Ages Aw*.

83

See how loose Nature, in respect
To her, it self doth recollect;
And every thing so whisht and fine,
Starts forth with to its *Bonne Mine*.
The *Sun* himself, of *Her* aware,
Seems to descend with greater Care;
And lest *She* see him go to Bed;
In blushing Clouds conceales his Head.

84

So when the Shadows laid asleep
From underneath these Banks do creep,
And on the River as it flows

With *Eben Shuts*★ begin to close;
The modest *Halcyon* comes in sight,
Flying betwixt the Day and Night;
And such an horror calm and dumb,
Admiring Nature does benum.

85

The viscous Air, wheres'ere She★ fly,
Follows and sucks her Azure dy;
The gellying Stream compacts below,
If it might fix her shadow so;
The stupid Fishes hang, as plain
As *Flies* in *Chrystal* overt'ane;
And Men the silent *Scene* assist,★
Charm'd with the *Saphir-winged Mist*.

86

Maria such, and so doth hush
The *World*, and through the *Ev'ning* rush.
No new-born *Comet* such a Train
Draws through the Skie, nor Star new-slain.
For streight those giddy Rockets fail,
Which from the putrid Earth exhale,
But by her *Flames*, in *Heaven* try'd,
Nature is wholy *vitrifi'd*.

87

'Tis *She* that to these Gardens gave
That wondrous Beauty which they have;
She streightness on the Woods bestows;
To *Her* the Meadow sweetness owes;
Nothing could make the River be
So Chrystal-pure but only *She*;
She yet more Pure, Sweet, Streight, and Fair,
Then Gardens, Woods, Meads, Rivers are.

88

Therefore what first *She* on them spent,
They gratefully again present.
The Meadow Carpets where to tread;
The Garden Flow'rs to Crown *Her* Head;
And for a Glass the limpid Brook,
Where *She* may all *her* Beautyes look;
But, since *She* would not have them seen,
The Wood about *her* draws a Skreen.

89

For *She*, to higher Beauties rais'd,
Disdains to be for lesser prais'd.
She counts her Beauty to converse
In all the Languages as *hers*;
Nor yet in those *her self* imployes
But for the *Wisdome*, not the *Noyse*;
Nor yet that *Wisdome* would affect,
But as 'tis *Heavens Dialect*.

90

Blest Nymph! that couldst so soon prevent
Those *Trains*★ by Youth against thee meant;
Tears (watry Shot that pierce the Mind;)
And *Sighs* (Loves Cannon charg'd with Wind;)
True Praise (That breaks through all defence;)
And *feign'd complying Innocence*;
But knowing where this *Ambush* lay,
She scap'd the safe, but roughest Way.

91

This 'tis to have been from the first
In a *Domestick Heaven* nurst,
Under the *Discipline* severe

Upon Appleton House, to my Lord Fairfax

Of *Fairfax*, and the starry *Vere*;
Where not one object can come nigh
But pure, and spotless as the Eye;
And *Goodness* doth it self intail
On *Females*, if there want a *Male*.

92

Go now fond Sex that on your Face
Do all your useless Study place,
Nor once at Vice your Brows dare knit
Lest the smooth Forehead wrinkled sit:
Yet your own Face shall at you grin,
Thorough the Black-bag* of your Skin;
When *knowledge* only could have fill'd
And *Virtue* all those *Furrows till'd*.

93

Hence *She* with Graces more divine
Supplies beyond her *Sex* the *Line*;
And, like a *sprig of Misleto*,
On the *Fairfacian Oak* does grow;
Whence, for some universal good,
The *Priest* shall cut the sacred Bud;
While her *glad Parents* most rejoice,
And make their *Destiny* their *Choice*.

94

Mean time ye Fields, Springs, Bushes, Flow'rs,
Where yet She leads her studious Hours,
(Till Fate her worthily translates,
And find a *Fairfax* for our *Thwaites*)
Employ the means you have by Her,
And in your kind your selves preferr;
That, as all *Virgins* She preceds,
So you all *Woods, Streams, Gardens, Meads*.

95

For you *Thessalian Tempe's Seat*
Shall now be scorn'd as obsolete;
Aranjuez,★ as less, disdain'd;
The *Bel-Retiro*★ as constrain'd;
But name not the *Idalian Grove,*
For 'twas the Seat of wanton Love;
Much less the Dead's *Elysian Fields,*
Yet nor to them your Beauty yields.

96

'Tis not, what once it was, the *World;*★
But a rude heap together hurl'd;
All negligently overthrown,
Gulfes, Deserts, Precipices, Stone.
Your lesser *World* contains the same.
But in more decent Order tame.
You Heaven's Center, Nature's Lap.
And Paradice's only Map.

97

But now the *Salmon-Fishers* moist
Their *Leathern Boats* begin to hoist;
And, like *Antipodes* in Shoes,
Have shod their *Heads* in their *Canoos.*
How *Tortoise like,* but not so slow,
These rational *Amphibii* go?
Let's in: for the dark *Hemisphere*
Does now like one of them appear.

Fleckno, an English Priest at Rome

Oblig'd by frequent visits of this man,
Whom as Priest, Poet, and Musician,
I for some branch of *Melchizedeck* took,
(Though he derives himself from *my Lord Brooke*⋆)
I sought his Lodging; which is at the Sign
Of the sad *Pelican*; Subject divine
For Poetry: There three Stair-Cases high,
Which signifies his triple property,
I found at last a Chamber, as 'twas said,
But seem'd a Coffin set on the Stairs head.
Not higher then Seav'n, nor larger then three feet;
Only there was nor Seeling, nor a Sheet,⋆
Save that th' ingenious Door did as you come
Turn in, and shew to Wainscot half the Room.
Yet of his State no man could have complain'd;
There being no Bed where he entertain'd:
And though within one Cell so narrow pent,
He'd *Stanza's* for a whole Appartement.⋆

    Straight without further information,
In hideous verse, he, and a dismal tone,
Begins to exercise;⋆ as if I were
Possest; and sure the *Devil* brought me there.
But I, who now imagin'd my self brought
To my last Tryal, in a serious thought
Calm'd the disorders of my youthful Breast,
And to my Martyrdom prepared Rest.
Only this frail Ambition did remain,
The last distemper of the sober Brain,
That there had been some present to assure
The future Ages how I did indure:

And how I, silent, turn'd my burning Ear
Towards the Verse; and when that could not hear,
Held him the other; and unchanged yet,
Ask'd still for more, and pray'd him to repeat:
Till the Tyrant, weary to persecute,
Left off, and try'd t' allure me with his Lute.

Now as two Instruments, to the same key
Being tun'd by Art, if the one touched be
The other opposite as soon replies,
Mov'd by the Air and hidden Sympathies;
So while he with his gouty Fingers craules
Over the Lute, his murmuring Belly calls,
Whose hungry Guts to the same streightness twin'd
In Echo to the trembling Strings repin'd.

I, that perceiv'd now what his Musick ment,
Ask'd civilly if he had eat this Lent.
He answered yes; with such, and such an one.
For he has this of gen'rous, that alone
He never feeds; save only when he tryes
With gristly Tongue to dart the passing Flyes.
I ask'd if he eat flesh. And he, that was
So hungry that though ready to say *Mass*
Would break his fast before, said he was Sick,
And th' *Ordinance* was only Politick.
Nor was I longer to invite him Scant:
Happy at once to make him Protestant,
And Silent. Nothing now Dinner stay'd
But till he had himself a Body made.
I mean till he were drest: for else so thin
He stands, as if he only fed had been
With consecrated Wafers: and the *Host*
Hath sure more flesh and blood then he can boast.
This *Basso Relievo* of a Man,
Who as a Camel tall, yet easly can

The Needles Eye thread without any stich,*
(His only impossible is to be rich)
Lest his too suttle Body, growing rare,
Should leave his Soul to wander in the Air,
He therefore circumscribes himself in rimes;
And swaddled in's own papers seaven times,
Wears a close Jacket of poetick Buff,
With which he doth his third Dimension Stuff.
Thus armed underneath, he over all
Does make a primitive *Sotana** fall;
And above that yet casts an antick Cloak,
Worn at the first Counsel of *Antioch*;
Which by the *Jews* long hid, and Disesteem'd,
He heard of by Tradition, and redeem'd.
But were he not in this black habit deck't,
This half transparent Man would soon reflect
Each colour that he past by; and be seen,
As the *Chamelion*, yellow, blew, or green.

He drest, and ready to disfurnish* now
His Chamber, whose compactness did allow
No empty place for complementing doubt,
But who came last is forc'd first to go out;
I meet one on the Stairs who made me stand,
Stopping the passage, and did him demand:
I answer'd he is here *Sir*; but you see
You cannot pass to him but thorow me.
He thought himself affronted; and reply'd,
I whom the Pallace never has deny'd
Will make the way here; I said *Sir* you'l do
Me a great favour, for I seek to go.
He gathring fury still made sign to draw;
But himself there clos'd in a Scabbard saw
As narrow as his Sword's; and I, that was
Delightful,* said there can no Body pass

Except by penetration* hither, where
Two make a crowd, nor can three Persons here
Consist but in one substance. Then, to fit
Our peace, the Priest said I too had some wit:
To prov't, I said, the place doth us invite
By its own narrowness, Sir, to unite.
He ask'd me pardon; and to make me way
Went down, as I him follow'd to obey.
But the propitiatory Priest had straight
Oblig'd us, when below, to celebrate
Together our attonement: so increas'd
Betwixt us two the Dinner to a Feast.

    Let it suffice that we could eat in peace;
And that both Poems did and Quarrels cease
During the Table; though my new made Friend
Did, as he threatned, ere 'twere long intend
To be both witty and valiant: I loth,
Said 'twas too late, he was already both.

    But now, Alas, my first Tormentor came,
Who satisfy'd with eating, but not tame
Turns to recite; though Judges most severe
After th'Assizes dinner mild appear,
And on full stomach do condemn but few:
Yet he more strict my sentence doth renew;
And draws out of the black box of his Breast
Ten quire of paper in which he was drest.
Yet that which was a greater cruelty
Then *Nero's* Poem he calls charity:
And so the *Pelican* at his door hung
Picks out the tender bosome to its young.

    Of all his Poems there he stands ungirt
Save only two foul copies for his shirt:
Yet these he promises as soon as clean.
But how I loath'd to see my Neighbour glean

Those papers, which he pilled* from within
Like white fleaks rising from a Leaper's skin!
More odious then those raggs which the *French* youth
At ordinaries after dinner show'th,
When they compare their *Chancres* and *Poulains*.
Yet he first kist them, and after takes pains
To read; and then, because he understood
Not one Word, thought and swore that they were good.
But all his praises could not now appease
The provok't Author, whom it did displease
To hear his Verses, by so just a curse
That were ill made condemn'd to be read worse:
And how (impossible) he made yet more
Absurdityes in them then were before.
For he his untun'd voice did fall or raise
As a deaf Man upon a Viol playes,
Making the half points and the periods run
Confus'der then the atomes in the Sun.
Thereat the Poet swell'd, with anger full,
And roar'd out, like *Perillus** in's own *Bull*;
Sir you read false. That any one but you
Should know the contrary.* Whereat, I, now
Made Mediator, in my room, said, Why?
To say that you read false *Sir* is no Lye.*
Thereat the waxen Youth relented straight;
But saw with sad dispair that 'twas too late.
For the disdainful Poet was retir'd
Home, his most furious Satyr to have fir'd
Against the Rebel; who, at this struck dead,
Wept bitterly as disinherited.
Who should commend his Mistress now? Or who
Praise him? both difficult indeed to do
With truth. I counsell'd him to go in time,
Ere the fierce Poets anger turn'd to rime.

Fleckno, an English Priest at Rome

He hasted; and I, finding my self free,
As one scap't strangely from Captivity,
Have made the Chance be painted; and go now
To hang it in *Saint Peter's* for a Vow.

An Horatian Ode upon Cromwel's
Return from Ireland*

The forward Youth that would appear
Must now*forsake his *Muses* dear,
   Nor in the Shadows sing
   His Numbers languishing.
'Tis time to leave the Books in dust,
And oyl th' unused Armours rust:
   Removing from the Wall
   The Corslet of the Hall.*
So restless *Cromwel* could not cease
In the inglorious Arts of Peace,
   But through adventrous War
   Urged his active Star.
And, like the three-fork'd Lightning, first
Breaking the Clouds where it was nurst,
   Did thorough his own Side*
   His fiery way divide.
For 'tis all one to Courage high
The Emulous or Enemy;
   And with such to inclose
   Is more then to oppose.*
Then burning through the Air he went,
And Pallaces and Temples rent:
   And *Cæsars* head at last
   Did through his Laurels* blast.
'Tis Madness to resist or blame
The force of angry Heavens flame:
   And, if we would speak true,
   Much to the Man is due.
Who, from his private Gardens, where
He liv'd reserved and austere,

As if his highest plot
To plant the Bergamot,★
Could by industrious Valour climbe
To ruine the great Work of Time,
   And cast the Kingdome old
   Into another Mold.
Though Justice against Fate complain,
And plead the antient Rights in vain:
   But those do hold or break
   As Men are strong or weak.
Nature that hateth emptiness,
Allows of penetration★ less:
   And therefore must make room
   Where greater Spirits come.
What Field of all the Civil Wars
Where his were not the deepest Scars?
   And *Hampton* shows what part
   He had of wiser Art.
Where, twining subtile★ fears with hope,
He wove a Net of such a scope,
   That *Charles* himself might chase
   To *Caresbrooks* narrow case.★
That thence the *Royal Actor* born
The *Tragick Scaffold* might adorn:
   While round the armed Bands
   Did clap their bloody hands.
He nothing common did or mean
Upon that memorable Scene:
   But with his keener Eye
   The Axes edge did try:
Nor call'd the *Gods* with vulgar spight
To vindicate his helpless Right,
   But bow'd his comely Head,
   Down as upon a Bed.

This was that memorable Hour
Which first assur'd the forced* Pow'r.
  So when they did design
  The *Capitols* first Line,
A bleeding Head where they begun,
Did fright the Architects to run;
  And yet in that the *State*
  Foresaw it's happy Fate.
And now the *Irish* are asham'd
To see themselves in one Year* tam'd:
  So much one Man can do,
  That does both act and know.
They can affirm his Praises best,
And have, though overcome, confest*
  How good he is, how just,
  And fit for highest Trust:
Nor yet grown stiffer with Command,
But still in the *Republick's* hand:
  How fit he is to sway
  That can so well obey.
He to the *Commons Feet* presents
A *Kingdome*, for his first years rents:
  And, what he may, forbears
  His Fame to make it theirs:
And has his Sword and Spoyls ungirt,
To lay them at the *Publick's* skirt.
  So when the Falcon high
  Falls heavy from the Sky,
She, having kill'd, no more does search,
But on the next green Bow to pearch;
  Where, when he first does lure,
  The Falckner has her sure.
What may not then our *Isle* presume
While Victory his Crest does plume!

What may not others fear
If thus he crown each Year!
A *Cæsar* he ere long to *Gaul*,
To *Italy* an *Hannibal*,
 And to all States not free
 Shall *Clymacterick** be.
The *Pict* no shelter now shall find
Within his party-colour'd Mind;
 But from this Valour sad*
 Shrink underneath the Plad:
Happy if in the tufted brake
The *English Hunter* him mistake;*
 Nor lay his Hounds in near
 The *Caledonian* Deer.
But thou the Wars and Fortunes Son
March indefatigably on;
 And for the last effect
 Still keep thy Sword erect:
Besides the force it has to fright
The Spirits of the shady Night,*
 The same *Arts* that did *gain*
 A *Pow'r* must it *maintain*.

Tom May's Death*

As one put drunk* into the Packet-boat,
Tom May was hurry'd hence and did not know't.
But was amaz'd on the Elysian side,
And with an Eye uncertain, gazing wide,
Could not determine in what place he was,
For whence in Stevens ally* Trees or Grass?
Nor where the Popes head, nor the Mitre lay,*
Signs by which still he found and lost his way.
At last while doubtfully he all compares,
He saw near hand, as he imagin'd *Ares*.*
Such did he seem for corpulence and port,
But 'twas a man much of another sort;
'Twas *Ben* that in the dusky Laurel shade
Amongst the Chorus of old Poets laid,
Sounding of ancient Heroes, such as were
The Subjects Safety, and the Rebel's Fear.
But how a double headed Vulture Eats,
Brutus and *Cassius* the Peoples cheats.
But seeing *May* he varied streight his Song,
Gently to signifie that he was wrong.
Cups more then civil of *Emathian* wine,
I sing (said he) and the *Pharsalian* Sign,
Where the Historian of the Common-wealth
In his own Bowels sheath'd the conquering health *
By this *May* to himself and them was come,
He found he was translated, and by whom.*
Yet then with foot as stumbling as his tongue*
Prest for his place among the Learned throng.
But *Ben*, who knew not neither foe nor friend,*
Sworn Enemy to all that do pretend,

Rose more then ever he was seen severe,
Shook his gray locks, and his own Bayes did tear
At this intrusion. Then with Laurel wand,
The awful Sign of his supream command.
At whose dread Whisk *Virgil* himself does quake,
And *Horace* patiently its stroke does take,
As he crowds in he whipt him ore the pate
Like *Pembroke* at the Masque, and then did rate.*
  Far from these blessed shades tread back agen
Most servil' wit, and Mercenary Pen.
*Polydore,** *Lucan, Allan,** *Vandale, Goth,*
Malignant Poet and Historian both.
Go seek the novice Statesmen, and obtrude
On them some Romane cast similitude,
Tell them of Liberty, the Stories fine,
Until you all grow Consuls in your wine.
Or thou *Dictator* of the glass bestow
On him the *Cato*, this the *Cicero.**
Transferring old *Rome* hither in your talk,
As *Bethlem's* House did to *Loretto* walk.*
Foul Architect that hadst not Eye to see
How ill the measures of these States agree.
And who by *Romes* example *England* lay,
Those but to *Lucan* do continue *May.**
But the nor Ignorance nor seeming good
Misled, but malice fixt and understood.
Because some one than thee more worthy weares
The sacred Laurel, hence are all these teares?
Must therefore all the World be set on flame,
Because a Gazet writer mist his aim?
And for a Tankard-bearing Muse must we
As for the Basket* *Guelphs* and *Gibellines* be?
When the Sword glitters ore the Judges head,

Tom May's Death

And fear has Coward Churchmen silenced,
Then is the Poets time, 'tis then he drawes,
And single fights forsaken Vertues cause.
He, when the wheel of Empire, whirleth back,
And though the World's disjointed Axel crack,
Sings still of ancient Rights and better Times,
Seeks wretched good, arraigns successful Crimes.
But thou base man first prostituted hast
Our spotless knowledge and the studies chast.
Apostatizing from our Arts and us,
To turn the Chronicler to *Spartacus*.
Yet wast thou taken hence with equal fate,
Before thou couldst great *Charles* his death relate.★
But what will deeper wound thy little mind,
Has left surviving *Davenant* still behind
Who laughs to see in this thy death renew'd,
Right Romane poverty and gratitude.
Poor Poet thou, and grateful Senate they,
Who thy last Reckoning did so largely pay.★
And with the publick gravity would come,
When thou hadst drunk thy last to lead thee home.
If that can be thy home where *Spencer* lyes
And reverend *Chaucer*, but their dust does rise
Against thee, and expels thee from their side,
As th' Eagles Plumes from other birds divide.★
Nor here thy shade must dwell, Return, Return,
Where Sulphrey *Phlegeton* does ever burn.
The *Cerebus* with all his Jawes shall gnash,
Megæra thee with all her Serpents lash.
Thou rivited unto *Ixion's* wheel
Shalt break, and the perpetual Vulture feel.
'Tis just what Torments Poets ere did feign,
Thou first Historically shouldst sustain.

Tom May's Death

Thus by irrevocable Sentence cast,
May only Master of these Revels past,
And streight he vanisht in a Cloud of pitch,
Such as unto the Sabboth bears the Witch.

To his worthy Friend Doctor Witty upon his
Translation of the Popular Errors*

Sit further, and make room for thine own fame,
Where just desert enrolles thy honour'd Name*
The good Interpreter. Some in this task
Take off the Cypress* vail, but leave a mask,
Changing the Latine, but do more obscure
That sence in *English* which was bright and pure.
So of Translators they are Authors grown,
For ill Translators make the Book their own.
Others do strive with words and forced phrase
To add such lustre, and so many rayes,
That but to make the Vessel shining, they
Much of the precious Metal rub away.
He is Translations thief that addeth more,
As much as he that taketh from the Store
Of the first Author. Here he maketh blots
That mends; and added beauties are but spots.
   *Cælia** whose English doth more richly flow
Then *Tagus*, purer then dissolved snow,
And sweet as are her lips that speak it, she
Now learns the tongues of *France* and *Italy*;
But she is *Cælia* still: no other grace
But her own smiles commend that lovely face;
Her native beauty's not Italianated,
Nor her chast mind into the *French* translated:
Her thoughts are *English*, though her sparkling wit
With other Language doth them fitly fit.
   Translators learn of her: but stay I slide
Down into Error with the Vulgar tide;
Women must not teach here: the Doctor doth
Stint them to Cawdles, Almond-milk,* and Broth.

123

To his worthy Friend Doctor Witty

Now I reform, and surely so will all
Whose happy Eyes on thy Translation fall,
I see the people hastning to thy Book,
Liking themselves the worse the more they look,
And so disliking, that they nothing see
Now worth the liking, but thy Book and thee.
And (if I Judgment have) I censure right;
For something guides my hand that I must write.
You have Translations statutes best fulfil'd.
That handling neither sully nor would guild.

The Character of Holland*

Holland, that scarce deserves the name of *Land*,
As but th'Off-scouring of the *Brittish Sand*;
And so much Earth as was contributed
By *English Pilots* when they heav'd the Lead;
Or what by th' Oceans slow alluvion* fell,
Of shipwrackt Cockle and the Muscle-shell;
This indigested vomit of the Sea
Fell to the *Dutch* by just Propriety.
   Glad then, as Miners that have found the Oar,
They with mad labour fish'd the *Land* to *Shoar*;
And div'd as desperately for each piece
Of Earth, as if't had been of *Ambergreece*,
Collecting anxiously small Loads of Clay,
Less then what building Swallows bear away;
Or then those Pills which sordid Beetles roul,
Transfusing into them their Dunghil Soul.
   How did they rivet, with Gigantick Piles,
Thorough the Center their new-catched Miles;
And to the stake a strugling Country bound,
Where barking Waves still bait the forced Ground;
Building their *watry Babel* far more high
To reach the *Sea*, then those to scale the *Sky*.
   Yet still his claim the Injur'd Ocean laid,
And oft at Leap-frog ore their Steeples plaid:
As if on purpose it on Land had come
To shew them what's their *Mare Liberum*.*
A daily deluge over them does boyl;
The Earth and Water play at *Level-coyl*;*
The Fish oft-times the Burger dispossest,
And sat not as a Meat but as a Guest;
And oft the *Tritons* and the *Sea-Nymphs* saw

Whole sholes of *Dutch* serv'd up for *Cabillau*;*
Or as they over the new Level rang'd
For pickled *Herring*, pickled *Heeren* chang'd.
Nature, it seem'd, asham'd of her mistake,
Would throw their Land away at *Duck* and *Drake*.*

   Therefore *Necessity*, that first made *Kings*,
Sometimes like *Government* among them brings.
For as with *Pygmees* who best kills the *Crane*,
Among the *hungry* he that treasures *Grain*,
Among the *blind* the one-ey'd *blinkard* reigns,
So rules among the *drowned* he that *draines*.
Not who first see the *rising Sun* commands,
But who could first discern the *rising Lands*.
Who best could know to pump an Earth so leak*
Him they their *Lord* and *Country's Father* speak.
To make a *Bank* was a great *Plot of State*;
Invent a *Shov'l* and be a *Magistrate*.
Hence some small *Dyke-grave*★ unperceiv'd invades
The *Pow'r*, and grows as 'twere a *King of Spades*.
But for less envy some *joynt States* endures,
Who look like a *Commission of the Sewers*.
For these *Half-anders*, half wet, and half dry,
Nor bear *strict service*, nor *pure Liberty*.

   'Tis probable *Religion* after this
Came next in order; which they could not miss.
How could the *Dutch* but be converted, when
Th' *Apostles* were so many Fishermen?
Besides the Waters of themselves did rise,
And, as their Land, so them did re-baptize.
Though *Herring* for their *God* few voices mist,
And *Poor-John*★ to have been th' *Evangelist*.
Faith, that could never Twins conceive before,
Never so fertile, spawn'd upon this shore:
More pregnant then their *Marg'ret*, that laid down*

126

The Character of Holland

For *Hans-in-Kelder*★ of a whole *Hans-Town*.
   Sure when *Religion* did it self imbark,
And from the *East* would *Westward* steer its Ark,
It struck, and splitting on this unknown ground,
Each one then pillag'd the first piece he found:
Hence *Amsterdam, Turk-Christian-Pagan- Jew,*
Staple of Sects and Mint of Schisme grew;
That *Bank of Conscience,* where not one so strange
Opinion but finds Credit, and Exchange.
In vain for *Catholicks* our selves we bear;
The *universal Church* is onely there.
Nor can Civility there want for *Tillage,*
Where wisely for their *Court* they chose a *Village.*★
How fit a Title clothes their *Governours,*
Themselves the *Hogs*★ as all their Subjects *Bores*!
   Let it suffice to give their Country Fame
That it had one *Civilis*★ call'd by Name,
Some Fifteen hundred and more years ago;
But surely never any that was so.
   See but their *Mairmaids* with their *Tails of Fish,*
Reeking at *Church* over the *Chafing-Dish.*
A vestal Turf enshrin'd in Earthen Ware
Fumes through the loop-holes of a wooden Square.
Each to the *Temple* with these *Altars* tend,
But still does place it at her *Western End;*
While the fat steam of *Female Sacrifice*
Fills the *Priests Nostrils* and puts out his *Eyes.*
   Or what a Spectacle the *Skipper gross,*
A Water-Hercules Butter-Coloss,★
Tunn'd up with all their sev'ral *Towns of Beer;*★
When Stagg'ring upon some Land, *Snick and Sneer,*★
They try, like Statuaries, if they can,
Cut out each others *Athos* to a Man:★
And carve in their large Bodies, where they please,

127

The Character of Holland

But when such Amity at home is show'd;
What then are their confederacies abroad?
Let this one court'sie witness all the rest;
When their whole Navy they together prest,
Not Christian Captives to redeem from Bands:
Or intercept the Western golden Sands:
No, but all ancient Rights and Leagues must vail,★
Rather then to the *English* strike their sail;
To whom their weather-beaten *Province* ows
It self, when as some greater Vessel tows
A Cock-boat tost with the same wind and fate;
We buoy'd so often up their *sinking State*.

Was this *Jus Belli & Pacis*;★ could this be
Cause why their *Burgomaster of the Sea*★
Ram'd with Gun-powder,★ flaming with Brand wine,★
Should raging hold his Linstock to the Mine?
While, with feign'd *Treaties*, they invade by stealth
Our sore new circumcised *Common wealth*.

Yet of his vain Attempt no more he sees
Then of *Case-Butter* shot and *Bullet-Cheese*.★
And the torn Navy stagger'd with him home,
While the Sea laught it self into a foam,
'Tis true since that (as fortune kindly★ sports,)
A wholesome Danger drove us to our Ports.★
While half their banish'd keels the Tempest tost,
Half bound at home in Prison to the frost:
That ours mean time at leizure might careen,
In a calm Winter, under Skies Serene.
As the obsequious Air and Waters rest,
Till the dear *Halcyon*★ hatch out all its nest.
The *Common wealth* doth by its losses grow;
And, like its own Seas, only Ebbs to flow.
Besides that very Agitation laves,

The Character of Holland

And purges out the corruptible waves.
   And now again our armed *Bucentore**
Doth yearly their* *Sea-Nuptials* restore.
And now the *Hydra of seaven Provinces*
Is strangled by our *Infant Hercules*.*
Their *Tortoise** wants its vainly stretched neck;
Their Navy all our Conquest or our Wreck:
Or, what is left, their *Carthage* overcome
Would render fain unto our better *Rome*.
Unless our *Senate*, lest their Youth disuse,
The War, (but who would) Peace if begg'd refuse.
   For now of nothing may our *State* despair,
Darling of Heaven, and of Men the Care;
Provided that they be what they have been,
Watchful abroad, and honest still within.
For while our *Neptune* doth a *Trident* shake,
Steel'd with those piercing Heads, *Dean, Monck and Blake*.
And while *Jove* governs in the highest Sphere,
Vainly in *Hell* let *Pluto* dominiceer.

The First Anniversary of the Government under O. C.*

Like the vain Curlings of the Watry maze,
Which in smooth streams a sinking Weight does raise;
So Man, declining alwayes, disappears
In the weak Circles of increasing Years;
And his short Tumults of themselves Compose,
While flowing Time above his Head does close.
    Cromwell alone with greater Vigour runs,
(Sun-like) the Stages of succeeding Suns:
And still the Day which he doth next restore,
Is the just Wonder of the Day before.
Cromwell alone doth with new Lustre spring,
And shines the Jewel of the yearly Ring.*
    'Tis he the force of scatter'd Time contracts,
And in one Year the work of Ages acts:
While heavy* Monarchs make a wide Return,
Longer, and more Malignant then *Saturn*:
And though they all *Platonique* years* should raign,
In the same Posture would be found again.
Their earthy Projects under ground they lay,
More slow and brittle then the *China* clay:
Well may they strive to leave them to their Son,
For one Thing never was by one King don.
Yet some more active for a Frontier Town
Took in by Proxie, beggs a false Renown;
Another triumphs at the publick Cost,
And will have Wonn, if he no more have Lost;
They fight by Others, but in Person wrong,
And only are against their Subjects strong;
Their other Wars seem but a feign'd contest,
This Common Enemy is still opprest;

If Conquerors, on them they turn their might;
If Conquered, on them they wreak their Spight:
They neither build the Temple in their dayes,
Nor Matter for succeeding Founders raise;
Nor sacred Prophecies consult within,
Much less themselves to perfect them begin;
No other care they bear of things above,
But with Astrologers divine, and *Jove*,
To know how long their Planet yet Reprives
From the deserved Fate their guilty lives:
Thus (Image-like)* an useless time they tell,
And with vain Scepter, strike the hourly Bell;
Nor more contribute to the state of Things,
Then wooden Heads unto the Viols strings.

    While indefatigable *Cromwell* hyes,
And cuts his way still nearer to the Skyes,
Learning a Musique in the Region clear,
To tune this lower to that higher Sphere.

    So when *Amphion* did the Lute command,
Which the God* gave him, with his gentle hand,
The rougher Stones, unto his Measures hew'd,
Dans'd up in order from the Quarreys rude;
This took a Lower, that an Higher place,
As he the Treble alter'd, or the Base:
No Note he struck, but a new Story lay'd,
And the great Work ascended while he play'd.

    The listning Structures he with Wonder ey'd,
And still new Stopps to various Time apply'd:
Now through the Strings a Martial rage he throws,
And joyning streight the *Theban* Tow'r arose;
Then as he strokes them with a Touch more sweet,
The flocking Marbles in a Palace meet;
But, for he most the graver Notes did try,
Therefore the Temples rear'd their Columns high:

Thus, ere he ceas'd, his sacred Lute creates
Th'harmonious City of the seven Gates.

Such was that wondrous Order and Consent,
When *Cromwell* tun'd the ruling Instrument;★
While tedious Statesmen many years did hack,
Framing a Liberty that still went back,★
Whose num'rous Gorge could swallow in an hour
That Island, which the Sea cannot devour:
Then our *Amphion* issues out and sings,
And once he struck, and twice, the pow'rful Strings.

The Commonwealth then first together came,
And each one enter'd in the willing Frame;
All other Matter yields, and may be rul'd;
But who the Minds of stubborn Men can build?
No Quarry bears a Stone so hardly wrought,
Nor with such labour from its Center brought;
None to be sunk in the Foundation bends,
Each in the House the highest Place contends,
And each the Hand that lays him will direct,
And some fall back upon the Architect;
Yet all compos'd by his attractive Song,
Into the Animated City throng.

The Common-wealth does through their Centers all★
Draw the Circumf'rence of the publique Wall;
The crossest Spirits here do take their part,
Fast'ning the Contignation★ which they thwart;
And they, whose Nature leads them to divide,
Uphold, this one, and that the other Side;
But the most Equal still sustein the Height,
And they as Pillars keep the Work upright;
While the resistance of opposed Minds,
The Fabrick as with Arches stronger binds,
Which on the Basis of a Senate free,
Knit by the Roofs Protecting weight★ agree.

The First Anniversary of the Government under O. C.

When for his Foot he thus a place had found
He hurles e'r since the World about him round;
And in his sev'ral Aspects, like a Star,
Here shines in Peace, and thither shoots a War.
While by his Beams observing Princes steer,
And wisely court the Influence they fear;
O would they rather by his Pattern won.
Kiss the approaching, nor yet angry Son;
And in their numbred Footsteps humbly tread
The path where holy Oracles do lead;*
How might they under such a Captain raise
The great Designes kept for the latter Dayes!
But mad with Reason, so miscall'd, of State
They know them not, and what they know not, hate.
Hence still they sing Hosanna to the Whore,
And her whom they should Massacre adore:
But Indians whom they should convert, subdue;
Nor teach, but traffique with, or burn the Jew.

Unhappy Princes, ignorantly bred,
By Malice some, by Errour more misled;
If gracious Heaven to my Life give length,
Leisure to Time, and to my Weakness Strength,
Then shall I once with graver Accents shake
Your Regal sloth, and your long Slumbers wake:
Like the shrill Huntsman that prevents the East,
Winding his Horn to Kings that chase the Beast.

Till then my Muse shall hollow far behind
Angelique *Cromwell* who outwings the wind;
And in dark Nights, and in cold Dayes alone
Pursues the Monster thorough every Throne:
Which shrinking to her *Roman* Den impure,
Gnashes her Goary teeth; nor there secure.

Hence oft I think, if in some happy Hour
High Grace should meet in one with highest Pow'r,

And then a seasonable People still
Should bend to his, as he to Heavens will,
What we might hope, what wonderful Effect
From such a wish'd Conjuncture might reflect.
Sure, the mysterious Work, where none withstand,
Would forthwith finish under such a Hand:
Fore-shortned Time its useless Course would stay,
And soon precipitate the latest Day.
But a thick Cloud about that Morning lyes,
And intercepts the Beams of Mortal eyes,
That 'tis the most which we determine can,
If these the Times, then this must be the Man.
And well he therefore does, and well has guest,
Who in his Age has always forward prest:
And knowing not where Heavens choice may light,
Girds yet his Sword, and ready stands to fight;
But Men alas, as if they nothing car'd,
Look on, all unconcern'd, or unprepar'd;
And Stars still fall, and still the Dragons Tail
Swinges the Volumes of its horrid Flail.
For the great Justice that did first suspend★
The World by Sin, does by the same extend.
Hence that blest Day still counterpoysed wastes,
The Ill delaying, what th'Elected hastes;
Hence landing Nature to new Seas is tost,
And good Designes still with their Authors lost.
     And thou, great *Cromwell*, for whose happy birth
A Mold was chosen out of better Earth;
Whose Saint-like Mother we did lately see★
Live out an Age, long as a Pedigree;
That she might seem, could we the Fall dispute,
T'have smelt the Blossome, and not eat the Fruit;
Though none does of more lasting Parents grow,
But never any did them Honor so;

The First Anniversary of the Government under O. C.

Though thou thine Heart from Evil still unstain'd,
And always hast thy Tongue from fraud refrain'd;
Thou, who so oft through Storms of thundring Lead
Hast born securely thine undaunted Head,
Thy Brest through ponyarding Conspiracies,
Drawn from the Sheath of lying Prophecies;★
Thee proof beyond all other Force or Skill,
Our Sins endanger, and shall one day kill.
    How near they fail'd, and in thy sudden Fall
At once assay'd to overturn us all.
Our brutish fury★ strugling to be Free,
Hurry'd thy Horses while they hurry'd thee.
When thou hadst almost quit thy Mortal cares,
And soyl'd in Dust thy Crown of silver Hairs.
Let this one Sorrow interweave among
The other Glories of our yearly★ Song.
Like skilful Looms which through the costly thred
Of purling★ Ore, a shining wave do shed:
So shall the Tears we on past Grief employ,
Still as they trickle, glitter in our Joy.
So with more Modesty we may be True,
And speak as of the Dead the Praises due:
While impious Men deceiv'd with pleasure short,
On their own Hopes shall find the Fall retort.
But the poor Beasts wanting their noble Guide,
What could they more? shrunk guiltily aside.
First winged Fear transports them far away,
And leaden Sorrow then their flight did stay.
See how they each his towring Crest abate,
And the green Grass, and their known Mangers hate,
Nor through wide Nostrils snuffe the wanton air,
Nor their round Hoofs, or curled Mane's compare;
With wandring Eyes, and restless Ears they stood,
And with shrill Neighings ask'd him of the Wood.

135

Thou *Cromwell* falling, not a stupid Tree,
Or Rock so savage, but it mourn'd for thee:
And all about was heard a Panique* groan,
As if that Natures self were overthrown.
It seem'd the Earth did from the Center* tear;
It seem'd the Sun was faln out of the Sphere:
Justice obstructed lay, and Reason fool'd;
Courage disheartned, and Religion cool'd.
A dismal Silence through the Palace went,
And then loud Shreeks the vaulted Marbles rent.
Such as the dying Chorus sings by turns,
And to deaf Seas, and ruthless Tempests mourns,
When now they sink, and now the plundring Streams
Break up each Deck, and rip the Oaken seams.

*But thee triumphant hence the firy Carr,
And firy Steeds had born out of the Warr,
From the low World, and thankless Men above,
Unto the Kingdom blest of Peace and Love:
We only mourn'd our selves, in thine Ascent,
Whom thou hadst left beneath with Mantle rent.

For all delight of Life thou then didst lose,
When to Command, thou didst thy self Depose;
Resigning up thy Privacy so dear,
To turn the headstrong Peoples Charioteer;*
For to be *Cromwell* was a greater thing,
Then ought below, or yet above a King:
Therefore thou rather didst thy Self depress,
Yielding To rule, because it made thee Less.

For, neither didst thou from the first apply
Thy sober Spirit unto things too High,
But in thine own Fields exercisedst long,
An healthful Mind within a Body strong;
Till at the Seventh time thou in the Skyes,
As a small Cloud, like a Mans hand didst rise;

Then did thick Mists and Winds the air deform,
And down at last thou pow'rdst the fertile Storm;
Which to the thirsty Land did plenty bring,
But though forewarn'd, o'r-took and wet the King.*

What since* he did, an higher Force him push'd
Still from behind, and it before him rush'd,
Though undiscern'd among the tumult blind,
Who think those high Decrees by Man design'd.
'Twas Heav'n would not that his Pow'r should cease,
But walk still middle betwixt War and Peace;*
Choosing each Stone, and poysing every weight,
Trying the Measures of the Bredth and Height;
Here pulling down, and there erecting New,
Founding a firm State by Proportions true.

When *Gideon* so did from the War retreat,
Yet by the Conquest of two Kings grown great,
He on the Peace extends a Warlike power,
And *Is'rel* silent saw him rase the Tow'r;
And how he *Succoths* Elders durst suppress,
With Thorns and Briars of the Wilderness.
No King might ever such a Force have done;
Yet would not he be Lord, nor yet his Son.

Thou with the same strength, and an Heart as plain,
Didst (like thine Olive) still refuse to Reign;
Though why should others all thy Labor spoil,
And Brambles be anointed with thine Oyl,
Whose climbing Flame, without a timely stop,
Had quickly Levell'd* every Cedar's top.
Therefore first growing to thy self a Law,
Th'ambitious Shrubs thou in just time didst aw.*

So have I seen at Sea, when whirling Winds,
Hurry the Bark, but more the Seamens minds,
Who with mistaken Course salute the Sand,
And threat'ning Rocks misapprehend for Land;

While baleful *Tritons* to the shipwrack guide.
And Corposants★ along the Tacklings slide.
The Passengers all wearyed out before,
Giddy, and wishing for the fatal Shore;
Some lusty Mate, who with more careful Eye
Counted the Hours, and ev'ry Star did spy,
The Helm does from the artless Steersman strain,
And doubles back unto the safer Main.
What though a while they grumble discontent,
Saving himself he does their loss prevent.

'Tis not a Freedome, that where All command;
Nor Tyranny, where One does them withstand:
But who of both the Bounders knows to lay
Him as their Father must the State obey.

Thou, and thine House, like *Noah's* Eight★ did rest,
Left by the Wars Flood on the Mountains crest:
And the large Vale lay subject to thy Will,
Which thou but as an Husbandman wouldst Till:
And only didst for others plant the Vine
Of Liberty, not drunken with its Wine.

That sober Liberty which men may have,
That they enjoy, but more they vainly crave:
And such as to their Parents Tents do press,
May shew their own, not see his Nakedness.

Yet such a *Chammish*★ issue still does rage,
The Shame and Plague both of the Land and Age,
Who watch'd thy halting, and thy Fall★ deride,
Rejoycing when thy Foot had slipt aside;
That their new King★ might the fifth Scepter shake,
And make the World, by his Example, Quake:
Whose frantique Army should they want for Men
Might muster Heresies, so one were ten.★
What thy Misfortune, they the Spirit call,
And their Religion only is to Fall.

The First Anniversary of the Government under O. C.

Oh *Mahomet*! now couldst thou rise again,
Thy Falling-sickness should have made thee Reign,
While *Feake* and *Simpson* would in many a Tome,
Have writ the Comments of thy sacred Foame:
For soon thou mightst have past among their Rant*
Wer't but for thine unmoved Tulipant;*
As thou must needs have own'd them of thy band
For prophecies fit to be *Alcorand*.*

    Accursed Locusts, whom your King does spit
Out of the Center of th'unbottom'd Pit;
Wand'rers, Adult'rers, Lyers, *Munser's* rest,*
Sorcerers, Atheists, Jesuites, Possest;
You who the Scriptures and the Laws deface
With the same liberty as Points* and Lace;
Oh Race most hypocritically strict!
Bent to reduce us to the ancient Pict;
Well may you act the *Adam* and the *Eve*;*
Ay, and the Serpent too that did deceive.

    But the great Captain, now the danger's ore,
Makes you for his sake Tremble one fit more;
And, to your spight, returning yet alive
Does with himself all that is good revive.

    So when first Man did through the Morning new
See the bright Sun his shining Race pursue,
All day he follow'd with unwearied sight,
Pleas'd with that other World of moving Light;
But thought him when he miss'd his setting beams,
Sunk in the Hills, or plung'd below the Streams.
While dismal blacks* hung round the Universe,
And Stars (like Tapers) burn'd upon his Herse:
And Owls and Ravens with their screeching noyse
Did make the Fun'rals sadder by their Joyes.
His weeping Eyes the doleful Vigils keep,
Not knowing yet the Night was made for sleep:

Still to the West, where he him lost, he turn'd,
And with such accents, as Despairing, mourn'd:
Why did mine Eyes once see so bright a Ray;
Or why Day last no longer then a Day?
When streight the Sun behind him he descry'd,
Smiling serenely from the further side.

So while our Star that gives us Light and Heat,
Seem'd now a long and gloomy Night to threat,
Up from the other World his Flame he darts,★
And Princes shining through their windows starts;
Who their suspected Counsellors refuse,
And credulous Ambassadors accuse.

'Is this, said one, the Nation that we read
'Spent with both Wars,★ under a Captain dead?
'Yet rig a Navy while we dress us late;
'And ere we Dine, rase and rebuild their State.
'What Oaken Forrests, and what golden Mines!
'What Mints of Men, what Union of Designes!
'Unless their Ships, do, as their Fowle proceed
'Of shedding Leaves, that with their Ocean breed.★
'Theirs are not Ships, but rather Arks of War,
'And beaked Promontories sail'd from far;
'Of floting Islands a new Hatched Nest;
'A Fleet of Worlds, of other Worlds in quest;
'An hideous shole of wood-Leviathans,
'Arm'd with three Tire of brazen Hurricans;
'That through the Center★ shoot their thundring side
'And sink the Earth that does at Anchor ride.
'What refuge to escape them can be found,
'Whose watry Leaguers★ all the world surround?
'Needs must we all their Tributaries be,
'Whose Navies hold the Sluces of the Sea.
'The Ocean is the Fountain of Command,
'But that once took, we Captives are on Land.

'And those that have the Waters for their share,★
'Can quickly leave us neither Earth nor Air.
'Yet if through these our Fears could find a pass;
'Through double Oak, & lin'd with treble Brass;
'That one Man still, although but nam'd, alarms
'More then all Men, all Navies, and all Arms.
'Him, all the Day, Him, in late Nights I dread,
'And still his Sword seems hanging o're my head.
'The Nation had been ours, but his one Soul
'Moves the great Bulk, and animates the whole.
'He Secrecy with Number hath inchas'd,★
'Courage with Age, Maturity with Hast:
'The Valiants Terror, Riddle of the Wise;
'And still his Fauchion all our Knots unties.★
'Where did he learn those Arts that cost us dear?
'Where below Earth, or where above the Sphere?
'He seems a King by long Succession born,
'And yet the same to be a King does scorn.
'Abroad a King he seems, and something more,
'At Home a Subject on the equal Floor.
'O could I once him with our Title see,
'So should I hope yet he might Dye as wee.
'But let them write his Praise that love him best,
'It grieves me sore to have thus much confest.
    Pardon, great Prince, if thus their Fear or Spight
More then our Love and Duty do thee Right.
I yield, nor further will the Prize contend;
So that we both alike may miss our End:
While thou thy venerable Head dost raise
As far above their Malice as my Praise.
And as the *Angel* of our Commonweal,
Troubling the Waters, yearly★ mak'st them Heal.

On the Victory obtained by Blake over the Spaniards, in the Bay of Sanctacruze, in the Island of Teneriff. 1657*

Now does *Spains* Fleet her spatious wings unfold,
Leaves the new World and hastens for the old:
But though the wind was fair, they slowly swoome
Frayted with acted Guilt, and Guilt to come:
For this rich load, of which so proud they are,
Was rais'd by Tyranny, and rais'd for War;
Ever capatious Gallions womb was fill'd,
With what the Womb of wealthy Kingdomes yield,
The new Worlds wounded Intrails they had tore,
For wealth wherewith to wound the old once more.
Wealth which all others Avarice might cloy,
But yet in them caus'd as much fear, as Joy.
For now upon the Main, themselves they saw,
That boundless Empire, where you give the Law,
Of winds and waters rage, they fearful be,
But much more fearful are your Flags to see.
Day, that to those who sail upon the deep,
More wish't for, and more welcome is then sleep,
They dreaded to behold, Least the Sun's light,
With *English* Streamers, should salute their sight:
In thickest darkness they would choose to steer,
So that such darkness might suppress their fear;
At length theirs vanishes, and fortune smiles;
For they behold the sweet Canary Isles;
One of which doubtless is by Nature blest
Above both Worlds, since 'tis above the rest.
For least some Gloominess might stain her sky,
Trees there the duty of the Clouds supply;

On the Victory by Blake over the Spaniards

O noble Trust which Heaven on this Isle poures,
Fertile to be, yet never need her showres.
A happy People, which at once do gain
The benefits without the ills of rain.
Both health and profit, Fate cannot deny;
Where still the Earth is moist, the Air still dry;
The jarring Elements no discord know,
Fewel and Rain together kindly grow;
And coolness there, with heat doth never fight,
This only rules by day, and that by Night.
Your worth to all these Isles, a just right brings,
The best of Lands should have the best of Kings.
And these want nothing Heaven can afford,
Unless it be, the having you their Lord;
But this great want, will not a long one prove,
Your Conquering Sword will soon that want remove.
For *Spain* had better, Shee'l ere long confess,
Have broken all her Swords, then this one Peace,
Casting that League off, which she held so long,*
She cast off that which only made her strong.
Forces and art, she soon will feel, are vain,
Peace, against you, was the sole strength of *Spain*.
By that alone those Islands she secures,
Peace made them hers, but War will make them yours.
There the indulgent Soil that rich Grape breeds,
Which of the Gods the fancied drink exceeds;
They still do yield, such is their pretious mould,
All that is good, and are not curst with Gold.
With fatal Gold, for still where that does grow,
Neither the Soyl, nor People quiet know.
Which troubles men to raise it when 'tis Oar,
And when 'tis raised, does trouble them much more.
Ah, why was thither brought that cause of War,
Kind Nature had from thence remov'd so far.

On the Victory by Blake over the Spaniards

In vain doth she those Islands free from Ill,
If fortune can make guilty what she will.
But whilst I draw that Scene, where you ere long,
Shall conquests act, your present are unsung.

    For *Sanctacruze* the glad Fleet takes her way,
And safely there casts Anchor in the Bay.
Never so many with one joyful cry,
That place saluted, where they all must dye.
Deluded men! Fate with you did but sport,
You scap't the Sea, to perish in your Port.
'Twas more for *Englands* fame you should dye there,
Where you had most of strength, and least of fear.

    The Peek's proud height, the *Spaniards* all admire,
Yet in their brests, carry a pride much higher.
Onely to this vast hill a power is given,
At once both to Inhabit Earth and Heaven.
But this stupendious Prospect did not neer,
Make them admire, so much as they did fear.

    For here they met with news, which did produce,
A grief, above the cure of Grapes best juice.
They learn'd with Terrour, that nor Summers heat,
Nor Winters storms, had made your Fleet retreat.
To fight against such Foes, was vain they knew,
Which did the rage of Elements subdue.
Who on the Ocean that does horror give,
To all besides, triumphantly do live.

    With hast they therefore all their Gallions moar,
And flank with Cannon from the Neighbouring shore.
Forts, Lines, and Sconces all the Bay along,
They build and act all that can make them strong.

    Fond men who know not whilst such works they raise,
They only Labour to exalt your praise.
Yet they by restless toyl, became at Length,
So proud and confident of their made strength,

144

On the Victory by Blake over the Spaniards

That they with joy their boasting General heard,
Wish then for that assault he lately fear'd.
His wish he has, for now undaunted *Blake*,
With winged speed, for *Sanctacruze* does make.
For your renown, his conquering Fleet does ride,
Ore Seas as vast as is the *Spaniards* pride.
Whose Fleet and Trenches view'd, he soon did say,
We to their Strength are more oblig'd then they.
Wer't not for that, they from their Fate would run,
And a third World seek out our Armes to shun.
Those Forts, which there, so high and strong appear,
Do not so much suppress, as shew their fear.
Of Speedy Victory let no man doubt,
Our worst works past, now we have found them out.
Behold their Navy does at Anchor lye,
And they are ours, for now they cannot fly.

This said, the whole Fleet gave it their applause,
And all assumes your courage, in your cause.
That Bay they enter, which unto them owes,
The noblest wreaths, that Victory bestows.
Bold *Stainer* Leads, this Fleets design'd by fate,
To give him Lawrel, as the Last did Plate.

The Thund'ring Cannon now begins the Fight,
And though it be at Noon, creates a Night.
The Air was soon after the fight begun,
Far more enflam'd by it, then by the Sun.
Never so burning was that Climate known,
War turn'd the temperate, to the Torrid Zone.

Fate these two Fleets, between both Worlds had brought.
Who fight, as if for both those Worlds they fought.
Thousands of wayes, Thousands of men there dye,
Some Ships are sunk, some blown up in the skie.
Nature ne'r made Cedars so high aspire,
As Oakes did then, Urg'd by the active fire.

On the Victory by Blake over the Spaniards

Which by quick powders force, so high was sent,
That it return'd to its* own Element.
Torn Limbs some leagues into the Island fly,
Whilst others lower, in the Sea do lye.
Scarce souls from bodies sever'd are so far,
By death, as bodies there were by the War.
Th' all-seeing Sun, neer gaz'd on such a sight,
Two dreadful Navies there at Anchor Fight.
And neither have, or power, or will to fly,
There one must Conquer, or there both must dye.
Far different Motives yet, engag'd them thus,
Necessity did them, but Choice did us.

A choice which did the highest worth express,
And was attended by as high success.
For your resistless genious there did Raign,
By which we Laurels reapt ev'n on the Mayn.
So prosperous Stars, though absent to the sence,
Bless those they shine for, by their Influence.

Our Cannon now tears every Ship and Sconce,
And o're two Elements Triumphs at once.
Their Gallions sunk, their wealth the Sea does fill,
The only place where it can cause no Ill.

Ah would those Treasures which both Indies have,
Were buryed in as large, and deep a grave,
Wars chief support with them would buried be,
And the Land owe her peace unto the Sea.
Ages to come, your conquering Arms will bless,
There they destroy, what had destroy'd their Peace.
And in one War the present age may boast,
The certain seeds of many Wars are lost.

All the Foes Ships destroy'd, by Sea or fire,
Victorious *Blake*, does from the Bay retire,
His Seige of *Spain* he then again pursues,
And there first brings of his success the news;

On the Victory by Blake over the Spaniards

The saddest news that ere to *Spain* was brought,
Their rich Fleet sunk, and ours with Lawrel fraught.
Whilst fame in every place, her Trumpet blowes,
And tells the World, how much to you it owes.

Two Songs at the Marriage of the Lord Fauconberg and the Lady Mary Cromwell*

FIRST

Chorus. Endymion. Cynthia

Chorus

Th' *Astrologers* own Eyes are set,
And even Wolves the Sheep forget;
Only *this Shepheard*, late and soon,
Upon this Hill outwakes the *Moon*.
Heark how he sings, with sad delight,
Thorough the clear and silent Night.

ENDYMION

Cynthia, O Cynthia, turn thine Ear,
Nor scorn *Endymions* plaints to hear.
As we our Flocks, so you command
The fleecy Clouds with silver wand.

CYNTHIA

If thou a *Mortal*, rather sleep;
Of if a *Shepheard*, watch thy Sheep.

ENDYMION

The *Shepheard*, since he saw thine Eyes,
And *Sheep* are both thy *Sacrifice*.
Nor merits he a *Mortal's* name,
That burns with an *immortal Flame*.

CYNTHIA

I have enough for me to do,
Ruling the Waves that Ebb and flow.

ENDYMION

Since thou disdain'st not then to share
On Sublunary things thy care;
Rather restrain these double Seas,
Mine Eyes uncessant deluges.

CYNTHIA

My wakeful Lamp all night must move,
Securing their Repose above.

ENDYMION

If therefore thy resplendent Ray
Can make a Night more bright then Day;
Shine thorough this obscurer Brest,
With shades of deep Despair opprest.

Chorus

Courage, *Endymion*, boldly Woo,
*Anchises** was a *Shepheard* too;
Yet is *her younger Sister* laid
Sporting with him in *Ida's shade*:
    And *Cynthia*, though the strongest,
Seeks but the honour to have held out longest.

ENDYMION

Here unto *Latmos Top* I climbe:
How far below thine *Orbe* sublime?
O why, as well as Eyes to see,
Have I not Armes that reach to thee?

CYNTHIA

'Tis needless then that I refuse,
Would you but your own Reason use.

ENDYMION

Though I so high may not pretend,
It is the same so you descend.

CYNTHIA

These Stars would say I do them wrong,
Rivals each one for thee too strong.

ENDYMION

The Stars are fix'd unto their *Sphere*,
And cannot, though they would, come near.
Less Loves set of each others praise,
While *Stars* Eclypse by mixing Rayes.

CYNTHIA

That Cave is dark.

ENDYMION

        Then none can spy:
Or shine Thou there and 'tis the Sky.

Chorus

Joy to *Endymion*,
For he has *Cynthia's* favour won.
And *Jove* himself approves
With his serenest influence their Loves.
For he did never love to pair
His Progeny above the Air;
But to be honest, valiant, wise,
Makes *Mortals* matches fit for *Deityes*.

Marriage of Lord Fauconberg and Lady Mary Cromwell

SECOND SONG

Hobbinol. Phillis. Tomalin.

HOBBINOL

Phillis, Tomalin, away:
Never such a merry day.
For *the Northern Shepheards Son.*
Has *Menalca's daughter* won.

PHILLIS

Stay till I some flow'rs ha' ty'd
In a Garland for the Bride.

TOMALIN

If thou would'st a Garland bring,
Phillis you may wait the Spring:
They ha' chosen such an hour
When *She* is the only flow'r.

PHILLIS

Let's not then at least be seen
Without each a Sprig of Green.

HOBBINOL

Fear not; at *Menalca's Hall*
There is Bayes enough for all.
He when Young as we did graze,
But when Old he planted Bayes.

TOMALIN

Here *She* comes; but with a Look
Far more catching then my Hook.
'Twas those Eyes, I now dare swear,
Led our Lambs we knew not where.

HOBBINOL

Not our Lambs own Fleeces are
Curl'd so lovely as her Hair:
Nor our Sheep new Wash'd can be
Half so white or sweet as *She*.

PHILLIS

He so looks as fit to keep
Somewhat else then silly *Sheep*.

HOBBINOL

Come, lets in some Carol new
Pay to Love and Them their due.

ALL

Joy to that *happy Pair*,
Whose Hopes united banish our Despair.
What *Shepheard* could for Love pretend,
Whil'st all the *Nymphs* on *Damon's* choice attend?
What *Shepherdess* could hope to wed
Before *Marina's* turn were sped?
Now lesser Beauties may take place,
And meaner Virtues come in play;
While they,
Looking from high,
Shall grace
Our Flocks and us with a propitious Eye.
But what is most, the gentle Swain
No more shall need of Love complain;
But Virtue shall be Beauties hire,
And those be equal that have equal Fire.
Marina yields. Who dares be coy?
Or who despair, now *Damon* does enjoy?
Joy to that happy Pair,
Whose Hopes united banish our Despair.

152

A Poem upon the Death of O. C.★

That Providence which had so long the care
Of *Cromwell's* head, and numbered ev'ry hair,
Now in its self (the Glass where all appears)
Had seen the period of his golden Years:
And thenceforth onely did attend to trace,
What death might least so fair a Life deface.
    The People, which what most they fear esteem,
Death when more horrid so more noble deem;
And blame the last *Act*, like *Spectators* vain,
Unless the *Prince* whom they applaud be slain.
Nor Fate indeed can well refuse that right
To those that liv'd in War, to dye in Fight.
    But long his *Valour* none had left that could
Indanger him, or *Clemency* that would.
And he whom Nature all for Peace had made,
But angry Heaven unto War had sway'd,
And so less useful where he most desir'd,
For what he least affected was admir'd,
Deserved yet an End whose ev'ry part
Should speak the wondrous softness of his Heart.
    To *Love* and *Grief* the fatal Writ was sign'd;★
(Those nobler weaknesses of humane Mind,
From which those Powers that issu'd the Decree,
Although immortal, found they were not free.)
That they, to whom his Breast still open lyes,
In gentle Passions should his Death disguise:
And leave succeeding Ages cause to mourn,
As long as Grief shall weep, or Love shall burn.
    Streight does a slow and languishing Disease
Eliza,★ Natures and his darling, seize.
Her when an infant, taken with her Charms,

153

He oft would flourish in his mighty Arms;
And, lest their force the tender burthen wrong,
Slacken the vigour of his Muscles strong;
Then to the Mothers brest her softly move,
Which while she drain'd of Milk she fill'd with Love.
But as with riper Years her Virtue grew,
And ev'ry minute adds a Lustre new;
When with meridian height her Beauty shin'd,
And thorough that sparkled her fairer Mind;
When She with Smiles serene and Words discreet
His hidden Soul at ev'ry turn could meet;
Then might y' ha' daily his Affection spy'd,
Doubling that knot which Destiny had ty'd.
While they by sence, not knowing, comprehend
How on each other both their Fates depend.
With her each day the pleasing Hours he shares,
And at her Aspect calms his growing Cares;
Or with a Grandsire's joy her Children* sees
Hanging about her neck or at his knees.
Hold fast dear Infants, hold them both or none;
This will not stay when once the other's gone.

A silent fire now wasts those Limbs of Wax,
And him within his tortur'd Image racks.*
So the Flowr with'ring which the Garden crown'd,
The sad Root pines in secret under ground.
Each Groan he doubled and each Sigh he sigh'd,
Repeated over to the restless Night.
No trembling String compos'd to numbers new,
Answers the touch in Notes more sad more true.
She lest He grieve hides what She can her pains,
And He to lessen hers his Sorrow feigns:
Yet both perceiv'd, yet both conceal'd their Skills,
And so diminishing increast their ills:
That whether by each others grief they fell,

A Poem upon the Death of O. C.

Or on their own redoubled, none can tell.

And now *Eliza*'s purple Locks* were shorn,
Where She so long her *Fathers* fate had worn:
And frequent lightning to her Soul that flyes,*
Devides the Air, and opens all the Skyes:
And now his Life, suspended by her breath,
Ran out impetuously to hasting Death.
Like polish'd Mirrours, so his steely Brest
Had ev'ry figure of her woes exprest;
And with the damp of her last Gasps obscur'd,
Had drawn such staines as were not to be cur'd.
Fate could not either reach with single stroke,
But the dear Image fled the Mirrour broke.

Who now shall tell us more of mournful Swans,
Of Halcyons kind, or bleeding Pelicans?
No downy breast did ere so gently beat,
Or fan with airy plumes so soft an heat.
For he no duty by his height excus'd,
Nor though a *Prince* to be a *Man* refus'd:
But rather then in his *Eliza's* pain
Not love, not grieve, would neither live nor reign:
And in himself so oft immortal try'd,
Yet in compassion of another dy'd.

So have I seen a Vine, whose lasting Age
Of many a Winter hath surviv'd the rage.
Under whose shady tent Men ev'ry year
At its rich bloods expence their Sorrows chear,
If some dear branch where it extends its life
Chance to be prun'd by an untimely knife,
The Parent-Tree unto the Grief succeeds,
And through the Wound its vital humour bleeds;
Trickling in watry drops, whose flowing shape
Weeps that it falls ere fix'd into a Grape.
So the dry Stock, no more that spreading Vine,

155

A Poem upon the Death of O. C.

Frustrates the Autumn and the hopes of Wine.

A secret Cause does sure those Signs ordain
Fore boding Princes falls, and seldom vain.
Whether some Kinder Pow'rs, that wish us well,
What they above cannot prevent, foretell;
Or the great World do by consent presage,
As hollow Seas with future Tempests rage:
Or rather Heav'n, which us so long foresees,
Their fun'rals celebrates while it decrees.
But never yet was any humane Fate
By nature solemniz'd with so much state.
He unconcern'd the dreadful passage crost;
But oh what pangs that Death did Nature cost!
First the great *Thunder* was shot off, and sent
The Signal from the starry Battlement.
The *Winds* receive it, and its force out-do,
As practising how they could thunder too:
Out of the Binders Hand the Sheaves they tore,
And thrash'd the Harvest in the airy floore;
Or of huge Trees, whose growth with his did rise,
The deep foundations open'd to the Skyes.
Then heavy *Showres* the winged Tempests lead,
And pour the Deluge ore the *Chaos* head.
The Race of warlike *Horses* at his Tomb
Offer themselves in many an *Hecatomb*;
With pensive head towards the ground they fall,
And helpless languish at the tainted Stall.
Numbers of *Men* decrease with pains unknown,*
And hasten not to see his Death their own.
Such Tortures all the Elements unfix'd,
Troubled to part where so exactly mix'd.
And as through Air his wasting Spirits flow'd,
The Universe labour'd beneath their load.

Nature it seem'd with him would Nature vye;*

156

A Poem upon the Death of O. C.

He with *Eliza*, It with him would dye.
   He without noise still travell'd to his End,
As silent Suns to meet the Night descend.
The *Stars* that for him fought had only pow'r
Left to determine now his fatal Hour;
Which, since they might not hinder, yet they cast*
To chuse it worthy of his *Glories* past.

   No part of time but bore his mark away
Of honour; all the Year was *Cromwell's* day:
But this, of all the most auspicious found,
Twice* had in open field him Victor crown'd:
When up the armed Mountains of *Dunbar*
He march'd, and through deep *Severn* ending war.
What day should him *eternize* but the same
That had before *immortaliz'd* his *Name*?
That so who ere would at his Death have joy'd,
In their own Griefs might find themselves imploy'd;
But those that sadly his departure griev'd,
Yet joy'd remembring what he once atchiev'd.
And the last minute his victorious *Ghost*
Gave chase to *Ligny* on the *Belgick Coast.**
Here ended all his mortal toyles: He lay'd
And slept in Peace under the *Lawrel** shade.

   O Cromwell, Heavens Favorite! To none
Have such high honours from above been shown:
For whom the Elements we Mourners see,
And *Heav'n* it self would the great Herald be;
Which with more Care set forth his Obsequies
Then those of *Moses* hid from humane Eyes;
As jealous only here lest all be less,
That we could to his Memory express.

   Then let us to our course of Mourning keep:
Where *Heaven* leads, 'tis *Piety* to weep.
Stand back ye Seas, and shrunk beneath the vail

A Poem upon the Death of O. C.

Of your Abysse, with cover'd Head bewail
Your *Monarch*: We demand not your supplies
To compass in our *Isle*; our Tears suffice;
Since him away the dismal Tempest rent,
Who once more joyn'd us to the Continent;
Who planted *England* on the *Flandrick shoar*,
And stretch'd *our frontire* to the *Indian Ore*;★
Whose greater *Truths* obscure the *Fables* old,
Whether of *British Saints or Worthy's*★ told;
And in a valour less'ning *Arthur's* deeds,
For Holyness the *Confessor* exceeds.

He first put Armes into *Religions* hand,
And tim'rous *Conscience* unto *Courage* man'd:
The Souldier taught that inward Mail to wear,
And *fearing God* how they should *nothing fear*.
Those Strokes he said will pierce through all below
Where those that strike from Heaven fetch their Blow.
Astonish'd armyes did their flight prepare,
And cityes strong were stormed by his prayer;
Of that for ever Preston's field shall tell★
The story, and impregnable Clonmell.
And where the sandy mountain Fenwick★ scal'd,
The sea between, yet hence his pray'r prevail'd.
What man was ever so in Heav'n obey'd
Since the commanded sun o're Gibeon stay'd?
In all his warrs needs must he triumph, when
He conquer'd God, still ere he fought with men:
Hence, though in battle none so brave or fierce,
Yet him the adverse steel could never pierce.
Pity it seem'd to hurt him more that felt
Each would himself which he to others delt;
Danger itself refusing to offend
So loose an enemy, so fast a friend.
Friendship, that sacred virtue, long dos claime

158

A Poem upon the Death of O. C.

The first foundation of his house and name:*
But within one its narrow limits fall,
His tendernesse extended unto all.*
And that deep soule through every channell flows,
Where kindly nature loves itself to lose.
More strong affections never reason serv'd,
Yet still affected most what best deserv'd.
If he Eliza lov'd to that degree,
(Though who more worthy to be lov'd than she?)
If so indulgent to his own, how deare
To him the children of the Highest were?
For her he once did nature's tribute pay:
For these his life adventur'd every day:
And 'twould be found, could we his thoughts have cast,
Their griefs struck deepest, if Eliza's last.
What prudence more than humane did he need
To keep so deare, so diff'ring minds agreed?
The worser sort, so conscious of their ill,
Lye weak and easy to the ruler's will;
But to the good (too many or too few)
All law is uselesse, all reward is due.
Oh! ill advis'd, if not for love, for shame,
Spare yet your own, if you neglect his fame;
Least others dare to think your zeale a maske,
And you to govern only Heaven's taske.
Valour, religion, friendship, prudence dy'd
At once with him, and all that's good beside;
And we death's refuse nature's dregs confin'd
To loathsome life, alas! are left behind.
Where we (so once we us'd) shall now no more,
To fetch day, presse about his chamber-door;
From which he issu'd with that awfull state,
It seem'd Mars broke through Janus' double gate;
Yet always temper'd with an aire so mild,

A Poem upon the Death of O. C.

No April sunns that e'er so gently smil'd;
No more shall heare that powerful language charm,
Whose force oft spar'd the labour of his arm:
No more shall follow where he spent the dayes
In warre, in counsell, or in pray'r, and praise;
Whose meanest acts he would himself advance,
As ungirt David to the arke did dance.
All, all is gone of ours or his delight
In horses fierce, wild deer, or armour bright;
Francisca* faire can nothing now but weep,
Nor with soft notes shall sing his cares asleep.

I saw him dead, a leaden slumber lyes,
And mortal sleep over those wakefull eyes:
Those gentle rays under the lids were fled,
Which through his looks that piercing sweetnesse shed;
That port which so majestique was and strong,
Loose and depriv'd of vigour, stretch'd along:
All wither'd, all discolour'd, pale and wan,
How much another thing, no more that man?
Oh! humane glory, vaine, oh! death, oh! wings,
Oh! worthlesse world! oh transitory things!
Yet dwelt that greatnesse in his shape decay'd,
That still though dead, greater than death he lay'd;
And in his alter'd face you something faigne
That threatens death, he yet will live again.
Not much unlike the sacred oak, which shoots
To Heav'n its branches, and through earth its roots:
Whose spacious boughs are hung with trophies round,
And honour'd wreaths have oft the victour crown'd.
When angry Jove darts lightning through the aire,
At mortalls sins, nor his own plant will spare;
(It groanes, and bruises all below that stood
So many yeares the shelter of the wood.)
The tree ere while foreshortned to our view,

A Poem upon the Death of O. C.

When fall'n shews taller yet than as it grew:
So shall his praise to after times encrease,
When truth shall be allow'd, and faction cease,
And his own shadows with him fall; the eye
Detracts from objects than itself more high:
But when death takes them from that envy'd seate,
Seeing how little we confess, how greate;
Thee, many ages hence, in martial verse
Shall th' English souldier, ere he charge, rehearse;
Singing of thee, inflame themselves to fight,
And with the name of Cromwell, armyes fright.
As long as rivers to the seas shall runne,
As long as Cynthia shall relieve the sunne,
While staggs shall fly unto the forests thick,
While sheep delight the grassy downs to pick,
As long as future time succeeds the past,
Always thy honour, praise and name, shall last.

Thou in a pitch how farre beyond the sphere
Of humane glory tow'rst, and raigning there
Despoyl'd of mortall robes, in seas of blisse,
Plunging dost bathe and tread the bright abysse:
There thy great soule at once a world does see,
Spacious enough, and pure enough for thee.
How soon thou Moses hast, and Joshua found,
And David, for the sword and harpe renown'd;
How streight canst to each happy mansion goe?
(Farr better known above than here below;)
And in those joyes dost spend the endlesse day,
Which in expressing, we ourselves betray.

For we, since thou art gone, with heavy doome,
Wander like ghosts about thy loved tombe;
And lost in tears, have neither sight nor mind
To guide us upward through this region blinde.
Since thou art gone, who best that way could'st teach,

A Poem upon the Death of O. C.

Onely our sighs, perhaps, may thither reach.
  And Richard* yet, where his great parent led,
Beats on the rugged track: he, vertue dead,
Revives; and by his milder beams assures;
And yet how much of them his griefe obscures.
He, as his father, long was kept from sight
In private, to be view'd by better light;
But open'd once, what splendour does he throw?
A Cromwell in an houre a prince will grow.
How he becomes that seat, how strongly streigns,
How gently winds at once the ruling reins?
Heav'n to this choice prepar'd a diadem,
Richer than any eastern silk, or gemme;
A pearly rainbow, where the sun inchas'd
His brows, like an imperiall jewell grac'd.
  We find already what those omens mean,
Earth ne'er more glad, nor Heaven more serene.
Cease now our griefs, calme peace succeeds a war,
Rainbows to storms, Richard to Oliver.
Tempt not his clemency to try his pow'r,
He threats no deluge, yet foretells a showre.

On Mr Milton's Paradise Lost*

When I beheld the Poet blind, yet bold,
In slender Book his vast Design unfold,
Messiah Crown'd, *Gods* Reconcil'd Decree,
Rebelling *Angels*, the Forbidden Tree,
Heav'n, Hell, Earth, Chaos, All; the Argument
Held me a while misdoubting his Intent,
That he would ruine (for I saw him strong)
The sacred Truths to Fable and old Song,
(So *Sampson** groap'd the Temples Posts in spight)
The World o'rewhelming to revenge his Sight.

   Yet as I read, soon growing less severe,
I lik'd his Project, the success did fear;
Through that wide Field how he his way should find
O're which lame Faith leads Understanding blind;
Lest he perplext the things he would explain,
And what was easie he should render vain.
   Or if a Work so infinite he spann'd,
Jealous I was that some less skilful hand*
(Such as disquiet alwayes what is well,
And by ill imitating would excell)
Might hence presume the whole Creations day
To change in Scenes, and show it in a Play.
   Pardon me, *mighty Poet*, nor despise
My causeless, yet not impious, surmise.
But I am now convinc'd, and none will dare
Within thy Labours to pretend a Share.
Thou hast not miss'd one thought that could be fit,
And all that was improper dost omit:
So that no room is here for Writers left,
But to detect their Ignorance or Theft.

On Mr Milton's Paradise Lost

That Majesty which through thy Work doth Reign
Draws the Devout, deterring the Profane.
And things divine thou treatst of in such state
As them preserves, and Thee inviolate.
At once delight and horrour on us seize,
Thou singst with so much gravity and ease;
And above humane flight dost soar aloft,
With Plume so strong, so equal, and so soft.
The *Bird* nam'd from that *Paradise*★ you sing
So never Flags, but alwaies keeps on Wing.

Where couldst thou Words of such a compass find?
Whence furnish such a vast expense of Mind?
Just Heav'n Thee, like *Tiresias*, to requite,
Rewards with *Prophesie* thy loss of Sight.

Well mightst thou scorn thy Readers to allure
With tinkling Rhime, of thy own Sense secure;
While the *Town-Bays*★ writes all the while and spells,
And like a Pack-Horse tires without his Bells.
Their Fancies like our bushy Points★ appear,
The Poets tag them; we for fashion wear.
I too transported by the *Mode* offend,
And while I meant to *Praise* thee, must Commend.
Thy verse created like thy *Theme* sublime,
In Number, Weight, and Measure, needs not *Rhime*.

Notes

18 *but:* only.
19 *fence The Batteries:* ward off the onslaughts.
20 *Center:* the centre of the Earth.
   Humility: by the degree of humility.
21 *For:* because of.
   incloses: the line may be paraphrased 'closes in on itself all round'.
   native Element: heaven.
   recollecting: collecting again.
   So the World excluding round: paraphrase 'thus shutting out the world on every side'.
22 *Congeal'd on Earth:* Exodus xvi. 21. 'And they gathered it morning by morning, every man according to his eating: and when the sun waxed hot, it melted.'
23 *Towers:* a very high head-dress worn by women.
   curious frame: elaborately wrought chaplet.
27 *Bermudas:* In July 1653 Marvell went to Eton as tutor to Cromwell's ward William Dutton, and lived with his pupil in the house of John Oxenbridge, Fellow of the College, who had twice visited the Bermudas.
   Unto an Isle so long unknown: they were discovered by Juan Bermudez in 1515.
   Where he . . . upon their Backs: the 'Battle' in Waller's poem is between the Bermudans and two stranded whales.
   Prelat: Laud. Oxenbridge was deprived by Laud of his tutorship at Magdalen Hall, Oxford, for reputedly exhibiting a contempt for college statutes.
   Ormus: Hormuz on the Persian Gulf.
   apples: pineapples, which the colonists introduced into the Bermudas.
32 *needless:* having no want.
34 *so:* with the murder forgotten by Heaven in accordance with my prayer.
   Deodands: things forfeited as having been responsible for a human death.
41 *dew:* warmth, in the sense of moisture and glow.
   slow-chapt pow'r: the power of his slowly-devouring jaws.
43 *bill:* peck.
   At sharp: with sharpened weapons.
44 *Banneret:* A knight dubbed on the battlefield.
45 *Examining:* testing.

Poems of Andrew Marvell

46 *And a Collection . . . or Mantua's were:* Charles I bought the entire cabinet of Vincenzo Gonzaga, Duke of Mantua, and added it to his great collection at Whitehall.

49 *molding:* either a substantive, the tears being mouldings of the eyes; or the participle of an intransitive verb, in which case *of* probably means *off*.

51 *compriz'd:* carried with it as a condition.

54 *For the Fern, whose magick Weed:* the reproduction of ferns not being understood they were believed to have an invisible seed. Gathered with due rites at midsummer-midnight it would make the bearer invisible.

58 *The Picture of little T.C. . . . :* 'Little T.C.' was possibly Theophila Cornewall.
   but: only.

62 *Luxurious:* in the seventeenth century meant voluptuous or lecherous.
   Onion root: during the tulip mania (at its height 1634–7) the bulbs were sold in Holland by weight like precious stones: a bulb of 10 grammes is recorded to have fetched 5,500 florins, i.e. 550 times the value of a sheep.
   Marvel of Peru: Mirabilis Jalapa, a plant.

64 *Juliana:* Gillian.
   hamstring'd: rendered inert by the heat.

67 *Shepherds-purse (Capsella Bursa-pastoris):* 'Shepheards purse stayeth bleeding in any part of the body, whether the iuyce or the decoction thereof be drunke, or whether it be used pultessewise, or any other way else.' Gerarde, Herball.
   Clowns-all-heal (Stachys palustris): 'Of Clownes Wound wort or All-heale. . . . The leaves hereof applied unto greene wounds in manner of a pultesse, healeth them in short time, and in such absolute manner, that it is hard for any that have not had the experience thereof to beleeve.' Gerarde, Herball.

68 *officious:* zealous, attentive.

69 *survey:* metaphor from a written survey of an estate.

74 *Oke:* the civic crown. *Bayes:* for poetry.
   but: only.

75 *curious:* exquisite.
   Annihilating . . . Thought: may be taken as meaning either 'reducing the whole material world to nothing material, i.e. to a green thought', or 'considering the whole material world as of no value compared to a green thought'.

76 *whets:* figuratively for 'preens'.

78 *For:* on account of.

79 *Vera:* Anne (d. 1665), daughter of Sir Horace Vere and wife of the great Lord Fairfax.

166

Notes

80 *this:* this Lord.

    Oak: i.e. at Dodona.

81 *Upon Appleton House:* The table overleaf may serve to illustrate the poem.

    The first Nun Appleton House was built on the lands of the Cistercian priory of Appleton (founded *c.* 1150), which passed to the Fairfaxes on its dissolution in 1542. A second was begun by the first Lord Fairfax in 1637 or 1638, which, though delayed by the war, was finished at about the time of the General's retirement in 1650. The Milner family pulled down the wings; the central part still stands. The meadows are still liable to flood, and the river still the resort of anglers. Some ruins of the nunnery still lie in the grounds south-east of the house, and the park, much thinner than in Marvell's day, still exists.

82 *loop:* as in loop-hole.

    Vere: Fairfax married in 1637 Anne, daughter of Sir Horace Vere, under whom he had served in the Low Countries.

    Romulus his Bee-like Cell: the traditional *casa Romuli,* a thatched hut (here compared with a beehive), was in antiquity preserved on the Palatine.

83 *Spherical:* the roof of the hall was 'spherical'.

    Frontispiece: decorated entrance.

    Mark of Grace: token of favour.

    Bishops Hill: within the walls of York on the right bank of the Ouse. The house of Bishop's Hill, where Mary Fairfax was born and Buckingham lived after his retirement, came into the family with Denton and Askwith as part of the inheritance of Isabel Thwaites. Denton lies on the left bank of the Wharfe about thirty miles above Nun Appleton.

84 *The Progress of this Houses Fate:* the heiress Isabel Thwaites, being wooed by William Fairfax of Steeton, was shut up by her guardian the Lady Anna Langton, Prioress of Nun Appleton; but an appeal was made to higher authority, she was released by force, and Fairfax married her in 1518. It was to their sons that the house was surrendered, it is said by the same Prioress, at its dissolution in 1542.

    white: the Cistercian habit is white.

85 *Yet thus:* even as you are.

87 *'Flow'rs dress . . . compose':* i.e. we lay up ambergris for the altar-cloths.

    griv'd: hurt in body.

88 *Now Fairfax . . . begin:* i.e. now claim her plighted word, from which religion (which she henceforward doth begin) has released her.

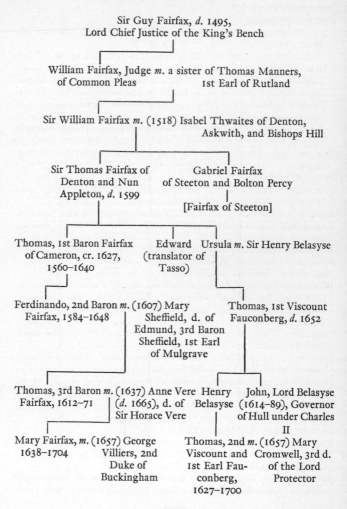

Sir Guy Fairfax, *d.* 1495,
Lord Chief Justice of the King's Bench

William Fairfax, Judge *m.* a sister of Thomas Manners,
of Common Pleas   1st Earl of Rutland

Sir William Fairfax *m.* (1518) Isabel Thwaites of Denton,
Askwith, and Bishops Hill

Sir Thomas Fairfax of   Gabriel Fairfax
Denton and Nun   of Steeton and Bolton Percy
Appleton, *d.* 1599

[Fairfax of Steeton]

Thomas, 1st Baron Fairfax   Edward   Ursula *m.* Sir Henry Belasyse
of Cameron, cr. 1627,   (translator of
1560–1640   Tasso)

Ferdinando, 2nd Baron *m.* (1607) Mary   Thomas, 1st Viscount
Fairfax, 1584–1648   Sheffield, d. of   Fauconberg, *d.* 1652
Edmund, 3rd Baron
Sheffield, 1st Earl
of Mulgrave

Thomas, 3rd Baron *m.* (1637) Anne Vere Henry   John, Lord Belasyse
Fairfax, 1612–71   (*d.* 1665), d. of Belasyse (1614–89), Governor
Sir Horace Vere   of Hull under Charles
II

Mary Fairfax, *m.* (1657) George   Thomas, 2nd *m.* (1657) Mary
1638–1704   Villiers, 2nd   Viscount and Cromwell, 3rd d.
Duke of   1st Earl Fau- of the Lord
Buckingham   conberg,   Protector
1627–1700

Notes

89 *state:* estate (property).

    Judge . . . Souldier: his father was Judge of Common Pleas, and his mother daughter of George Manners, 12th Lord Roos, a distinguished soldier who died at the siege of Tournay in 1513.

    Is not this he . . . Germany: Sir Thomas Fairfax (son of Sir William Fairfax and Isabel Thwaites) fought in Italy and Germany; his son Thomas, first Lord Fairfax, was knighted for gallantry before Rouen. Two sons of the first Lord Fairfax fell at Frankenthal in Germany, one died at Scanderoon in Turkey, and one after an affray with French soldiers in Paris. The Great Lord himself fought at Bois-le-Duc.

    vault: the bulk of the unborn scheme stretches the architect's brain till his skull serves for a model.

90 *disjointed:* distracted.

91 *From that blest . . . for ev'ry sense:* these lines would naturally refer to Sir Thomas Fairfax.

    Pan: the part of the musket-lock which held the priming.

    Flask: powder-flask.

    think . . . compare: imperatives addressed to the flowers (compare meaning to challenge comparison with).

93 *Switzers of our Guard:* the Swiss Guard at the Vatican still wears the uniform with black, yellow, and red stripes, of which the tulips reminded the poet.

    Cinque Ports: Fairfax was not Lord Warden of the Cinque Ports, though as commander-in-chief he had been responsible for their defence. But the Cinque Ports are introduced here chiefly to contrast with the five imaginary Forts.

    spann'd: limited.

    A prickling leaf . . . touch: the sensitive plant, 'Herba mimosa or the Mocking herbe' of which at least one variety is prickly.

94 *Cawood:* on the Ouse, two miles S.E. from Nun Appleton, a seat of the Archbishop of York, who fled from it in 1642.

    quarrell'd: transitive use, to find fault with.

    Whether he fall through it or go: whether he is going downwards or forwards.

    Scene: stage. The masques at the courts of James I and Charles I were performed with elaborate scenic effects.

95 *And crowd a Lane to either Side:* to crowd to either side to form a lane.

    Rail: landrail or corncrake.

    Sourdine: 'a kind of hoarse or low-sounding Trumpet,' Cotgrave.

96 *Hay:* also the name of a country dance.

    Smells like an Alexanders sweat: 'I remember I read also in the commentaries of Aristoxenus that his skin had a marvellous good savour, and

96 that his breath was very sweete: insomuch that his body had so
sweete a smell of it selfe, that all the apparell he wore next unto his
body took thereof a passing delightful savour, as it had been
perfumed.' North's Plutarch, *Alexander*.

97 *Lilly* (so spelt by Pepys): Sir Peter Lely, who came to England in 1641;
the cloth is his canvas.

Toril: The word now means the place where the bulls are shut up
before they are brought out for the bullfight. Marvell uses it for the
space cleared for the bullfight.

Madril: Madrid.

They seem . . . Looking-Glass: the reflection in the mirror appears to the
eye to be smaller than the landscape.

Such fleas . . . Glasses lye: fleas under glass preparatory to inspection by
a microscope appear mere dots on a wide surface, until looked at
through the microscope (ere they approach the Eye).

98 *How eels . . . Leeches quick:* the usual story is that eels are bred from
horses' hairs that have fallen into water.

Union I take to be subject: the two woods are joined at one point, just
as the Vere and Fairfax pedigrees are joined.

Of whom though many fell in War: some of the trees may have been felled
for purposes connected with the war.

Neighbourhood: nearness.

100 *Stork-like:* 'The Dutch held the belief that the stork, in leaving a house
where she had been encouraged to build, left one of her young ones
behind for the owner' (Phipson, *Animal-Lore of Shakespeare's Time*, p.272).

Hewel: the green woodpecker.

Holt-felsters: holt-fellers, i.e. woodcutters.

102 *Could with a Mask my studies hit:* could provide me with a masquing
habit suitable to my studies.

shed: separate, part, especially and frequently of the hair (now dialec-
tal); the meaning is 'Zephyrs, who blow through my hair and my
thoughts'.

103 *slick:* sleek.

104 *Quills:* floats.

105 *Shuts:* shutters.

She: the halycon.

assist: stand by.

106 *Trains:* of artillery.

107 *Yet your own Face . . . Skin:* It will be still your own face mocking the
efforts which have in fact spoiled your complexion.

Black-bag: mask.

Notes

108 *Aranjuez:* on the Tagus, thirty miles from Madrid. The lovely and famous gardens included the Jardin de la Isla, laid out for Philip II, who also planted the country with English elms.

Bel-Retiro: Buen Retiro, another royal residence near Madrid.

'Tis not, what once it was, the World: the world is no longer the world, since you created a new standard, it becomes by comparison a rude heap.

109 *my Lord Brooke:* the nature, real or imaginary of Flecknoe's connexion, with Lord Brooke is unknown. He dedicated to Lady Nevill Brooke in 1640 *The Affections of a Pious Soule, unto our Saviour-Christ.*

Seeling . . . Sheet: the passage is punning on the properties of the coffin and of the room. *Seeling* can mean wall-hangings; black hangings were used at funerals; and it means a wainscot. *Sheet* stands for a bed-sheet and a winding-sheet.

Stanza: in Italian, a room. *Appartement:* suite of rooms.

exercise: exorcize.

111 *stich:* grimace (of pain in getting through anything so narrow); also stitch (as in sewing).

Sotana: cassock.

disfurnish: i.e. of its occupants.

Delightful: delighted.

112 *penetration:* 'Penetration of dimensions' in natural philosophy was 'used for a supposed or conceived occupation of the same space by two bodies at the same time' (O.E.D.).

113 *pilled:* peeled.

Perillus: the contriver of the Brazen Bull of Phalaris and its first victim.

That . . . contrary: said by the man who had been reading.

is no Lye: is not to give you the lie (i.e. it is no occasion for a challenge).

115 *An Horatian Ode upon Cromwel's Return from Ireland:* Cromwell returned from Ireland at the end of May 1650, to take part in the Scottish campaign. Fairfax was appointed commander-in-chief on 12 June 1650, with Cromwell as his lieutenant-general; Fairfax resigned the appointment, as unwilling to lead an attack on Scotland unless provoked by an invasion; on 26 June Cromwell was made captain-general and commander-in-chief of the Parliamentary forces, and he entered Scotland on 22 July 1650.

now: the war for about a year before the probable date of the poem had been confined to Ireland. The call may be to the new war in the north, following the proclamation of Charles II and the raising of the Highlands by Montrose. These lines, however, suggesting as they do a longer period of peace, are possibly a fragment of earlier com-

171

115   position; or they may be read as an exhortation from the poet to himself (like many others he had taken no part in the fighting): or *now* may merely mean 'in these troublous days'.

    And oyl . . . of the Hall: describes what went on throughout the country in 1642.

    Side: (1) party. Cromwell's emergence from among the other Parliamentary leaders became marked at and after Marston Moor (1644). (2) The lightning is conceived as tearing through the side of its own body the cloud.

    And with such . . . to oppose: to shut in and cramp a man of high courage is worse (less tolerable for him) than to oppose him. That is why Cromwell burst through his own party.

    Laurels: it was believed that laurels were proof against lightning.

116   *Bergamot:* a fine kind of pear. Many new varieties of fruit-trees were introduced in the first half of the seventeenth century.

    penetration: See note to page 112.

    subtile: the original sense is *finely woven* as of a net.

    case: plight; with the alternative or additional sense of a cage. Charles I fled from Hampton Court 11 November 1647 to Carisbrooke, where he stayed till he was transferred to Hurst Castle, 1 December 1648.

117   *forced:* gained and maintained by force.

    one Year: Cromwell landed at Dublin on 15 August 1649.

    confest: Irish testimony in favour of Cromwell at this moment is highly improbable. Possibly there is a reference to the voluntary submission of part of Munster with its English colony.

118   *Clymacterick:* critical, marking an epoch.

    Sad: steadfast.

    mistake: because of his protective colouring.

    Besides the force . . . the shady Night: the cross-hilt of the sword would avert the *Spirits of the shady Night.*

119   *Tom May's Death:* Thomas May, 1595–1650, playwright, poet, historian, and translator of Lucan, made his reputation at the court of Charles I, and later attached himself to the Parliamentary cause, holding employment under the House of Commons. It appears that he had hoped to succeed Ben Jonson as poet laureate in 1637, and it was to chagrin at the appointment of Davenant that his enemies attributed the change in his political position. He died 13 November 1650. His body was removed from Westminster Abbey by warrant dated 9 September 1661 and his monument taken down. There is no trace of publication before 1681, and the text may represent a topical adaptation in 1661 of an earlier manuscript.

119 *drunk:* Aubrey says that May 'came of his death after drinking with his chin tyed with his cap (being fatt); suffocated'.

Stevens ally: Canon Row or St Stephen's Alley, Westminster, lay in the neighbourhood of King Street and Tothill Street; it was a well-known street of taverns.

Popes head . . . Mitre: these were common signs, besides providing a convenient innuendo for the satirist.

Ares: perhaps the keeper of a tavern frequented by May.

Cups more then civil . . . conquering health: May's translation of Lucan's *Pharsalia* begins:

> Warres more than civill on Æmathian plaines
> We sing; rage licensd; where great Rome distaines
> In her owne bowels her victorious swords; . . .

whom: Death. *translated* is a jocular allusion to the translator of Lucan.

Yet then with foot . . . as his tongue: Clarendon says that May suffered from 'an imperfection in his speech, which was a great mortification to him'.

friend. Ben Jonson addresses *Underwoods*, xxi, 'To my chosen friend, the learned Translator of Lucan, Thomas May, Esquire'.

120 *Like Pembroke at the Masque, and then did rate:* 'On *Monday* after *Candelmas-day*, the Gentlemen of the Inns of Court performed their Masque at Court. . . . They were well used at Court by the King and Queen, no Disgust given them, only this one Accident fell, Mr *May* of *Gray's Inn*, a fine Poet, he who translated *Lucan*, came athwart my Lord Chamberlain in the Banquetting House, and he broke his Staff over his Shoulders, not knowing who he was, the King present, who knew him, for he calls him his Poet, and told the Chamberlain of it, who sent for him the next Morning, and fairly excused himself to him, and gave him fifty Pounds in Pieces. I believe he was the more indulgent for his names sake' (Letter from G. Garrard to Strafford).

Polydore: Polydore Virgil (d. 1555), who wrote an *Historia Anglica* and was subsequently imprisoned for an attack on Henry VIII and Wolsey.

Allan. one of the Alani, a Scythian people mentioned in Lucan's *Pharsalia*, where May's translation is 'Unquiet Alans'. Their reputation was like that of the Vandals and Goths.

On him the Cato, this the Cicero: May's *History of the Parliament of England* contains numerous classical parallels.

As Bethlem's House did to Loretto walk: the Santa Casa of Loreto is venerated as the house of the Virgin, miraculously conveyed from Nazareth (not from Bethlehem) to Illyria in 1291, and finally to its present site.

120 *Those but to Lucan do continue May:* May produced a *Continuation of Lucan's Historicall Poem till the death of Julius Caesar.*

Basket: perhaps alludes to the borsa or bag which received the votes in Florentine elections, the scene of frequent fighting between Guelphs and Ghibellines.

121 *Before thou couldst great Charles his death relate:* May's *Breviary of the History of the Parliament of England* (1650) ends thus: 'But by what means, or what degrees, it came at last so far, as that the king was brought to trial, condemned, and beheaded: because the full search and narration of so great a business would make an History by itself, it cannot well be brought into this BREVIARY; which having passed over so long a time, shall here conclude.'

Who thy last Reckoning did so largely pay: The Council of State voted £100 to cover the expenses of May's burial in Westminster Abbey.

As th' Eagles Plumes from other birds divide: the feathers of eagles were supposed to have a corrosive power.

123 *To his worthy Friend Doctor Witty . . . :* This poem, together with a Latin version of it, appeared as commendatory verses to a work called *Popular Errours. Or the Errours of the People in Physick. First written in Latine by the learned Physitian James Primrose.*

Sit farther . . . thy honour'd Name: the translation has to make way for the commendatory verses.

Cypress: Cypress lawn.

Caelia: probably Mary Fairfax.

Cawdles: gruels. *Almond-milk:* a preparation of sweet almonds and water, used as an emollient.

125 *The Character of Holland:* Deane, Monk, and Blake held office together as Generals at sea from 26 November 1652 till Deane's death in action on 3 June 1653. It would appear from: 'Steel'd with those piercing Heads, *Dean, Monck and Blake*' that the *Character of Holland* was written during that time, probably (see *And now the Hydra . . . our Infant Hercules*) after the English victory over the Dutch fleet off Portland, 18–20 February 1653.

alluvion: legal term for the formation of new land by the water's action.

Mare Liberum: the title of a book by Grotius published in 1609. It was written against the Portuguese claim to private possession of Eastern waters; the doctrine gained importance later in the disputes between England and Holland about the English Channel. Selden in *Mare Clausum* (1632) set out to refute Grotius's doctrine of the freedom of the seas. The Commonwealth Government claimed the Channel as British, and required foreign ships to salute the English flag.

Notes

125 *Level-coyl* (level le cul): a boisterous game, in which each player was unseated in turn and succeeded by another.

126 *Cabillau:* cod-fish.

Duck and Drake: a game of making flat stones skim along the surface of the water.

leak: leaky.

Dyke-grave: officer in charge of the sea-walls in Holland.

Poor-John: dried hake.

More pregnant then . . . laid down: cf. Evelyn's *Diary* for 1 September 1641: 'I now rode out of town (The Hague) to see the monument of the woman, pretended to have been a countess of Holland, reputed to have had as many children at one birth, as there are days in the year. The basins were hung up in which they were baptized, together with a large description of the matter-of-fact in a frame of carved work, in the Church of Lyrdun.'

127 *Hans in Kelder* (Jack-in-the-cellar): child in the womb. *Hans-Town:* Hanse-town, member of the League.

Village: owing to the jealousy of the towns entitled to vote in the assembly of the States, The Hague was denied a voice in that body, and therefore continued to be 'the largest village in Europe', until Louis Bonaparte, when King of Holland, conferred on it the privileges of a town.

Hogs: Hoog-mogenden, high and mighty; the official title of the States-General. *Bores:* Boers.

Civilis: leader of the Batavi against the Romans, AD 69.

Butter-Coloss: the nickname Butter-box (butter-bag, butter-mouth) denoted a Dutchman.

Towns of Beer: several Dutch towns begin with Beer- or Bier-, e.g. Biervliet.

Snick and Sneer: a variant of snick and snee (thrust and cut).

They try, like Statuaries . . . to a Man: Deinocrates the sculptor proposed to carve Mount Athos into an effigy of Alexander.

128 *vail:* salute by lowering colours. 'Driven by stress of weather, as the Dutch afterwards explained, or from some whim of his own, he (Van Tromp) did appear, on the 19th of May (1652), in the Downs, off Dover. By good luck or ill luck, Blake had contrived to be thereabouts too; and, though he had but twenty-three ships (to Van Tromp's forty-two), he put himself sturdily in Van Tromp's way. A point of naval etiquette included in the English claims was that foreign ships in the narrow seas should lower their flags to the English, and Blake signalled to Van Tromp for this courtesy. Van

128   Tromp positively declined; and, as Blake dogged him and persisted he veered round, and sent a broadside into Blake's flagship. "Not very civil in Brother Tromp to break my windows," said Blake, and opened back, with all his might, on the Dutchman . . . The States General, however, hastened to repair Van Tromp's blunder, by immediately despatching to London a fourth Ambassador Extraordinary to offer apologies and explanations, and to assist the other three in pushing on the Treaty' (Masson, *Life of Milton*, iv. 372–3).

Jus Belli & Pacis: Grotius, *De jure belli et pacis*, was published in 1625.

Burgomaster of the Sea: Van Tromp.

Gun-powder: it 'was not uncommon for the older seadogs to drink "spirits" strengthened, as they supposed, with gun-powder' (Grosart).

Brand wine: brandy.

Case-Butter shot: canister shot, 'a collection of small projectiles put up in cases to fire from a cannon'. Van Tromp sees no more result than if he had used butter for case-shot and cheese for bullets.

kindly: in accordance with her nature.

A wholesome Danger drove us to our Ports: 'With but thirty-seven ships he (Blake) engaged Van Tromp's fleet of seventy-three in the Channel, on the 29th of November (1652), and fought with it the whole day, his own ship always in the thickest fire, from forenoon till night. Not successfully, however. Two of the English ships had been taken; Blake's ship, brought off a mere hull after having been twice boarded, had to seek shelter in English harbours with the rest of his battered ships and Van Tromp, in signal that he now swept the Channel, cruised about it with a broom at his mast-head.'

Halcyon: according to the ancients a fortnight's calm was created at about the winter solstice while the halcyon brooded on her floating nest.

129 *Bucentore:* Bucentaur, the State barge of the Venetian Republic, from which the *Sposalizio del Mar* was celebrated yearly on Ascension Day.

their: perhaps for 'our'.

And now . . . Infant Hercules: 'Hercules of old strangled snakes in his infancy, but destroyed the Hydra in his full strength. Our Hercules in his infancy strangles the Hydra.' The allusion is probably to the English victory off Portland Bill, 18–20 February 1653.

Tortoise: After all, the Dutch hydra was only a tortoise; its one neck has been cut by Blake.

130 *The First Anniversary of the Government under O.C.:* Cromwell was made Protector on 16 December 1653; this poem, written for December 1654, was published in the following year. Marvell was still, so far as

Notes

130   we know, at Eton in the capacity of tutor to Cromwell's protégé
      William Dutton.

the Jewel of the yearly Ring: Cromwell's crest was 'a demi-lion rampant
argent holding in the dexter paw a gem ring or'. It has been
suggested to me that, as the sun was the tutelar planet of the lion,
there is here 'a twist of heraldic and astrological figures'.

heavy: the metal associated with the unpropitious planet Saturn is lead.
Longer: the Saturnian was the longest known year before the dis-
covery of Uranus and Neptune.

Platonique years: opinions varied about the duration of the Platonic
Great Year (26,000 to 36,000 Solar years), but it was held by some
writers that, the heavenly bodies controlling the course of events,
each cycle would see an exact repetition of human history.

131   *Image-like:* like the clock-figures striking the hour on a bell.
      the God: Hermes.

132   *Instrument:* Cromwell's Protectorate was established by the Instrument
of Government, 1653.

While tedious Statesmen . . . still went back: refers to the attempts made
between 1649 and 1653 to frame a satisfactory Constitution.

The Common-wealth does through their Centers all: The Declaration 'shewing
the Reasons' why the Long Parliament was dissolved (April 1653)
announces the decision 'that the Supreme Government should be by
the Parliament devolved upon known persons . . . as the most
hopeful way to countenance all God's people . . .'

Contignation: (1) a framework, (2) a (timber) floor. The existence of an
opposition contributes to the union of the State just as a framework
is held together by the cross-pieces, or '*While the resistance . . .
Arches stronger binds'* as an arch is maintained by two opposing pressures.

the Roofs Protecting weight: the weight of the Protector's authority.

133   *O would they . . . Oracles do lead:* Ps. ii. 10–12. *numbred:* by the *holy
Oracles.* The whole of the passage which follows to '*And good Designes
still with their Authors lost.'* takes its colour from the apocalyptic
prophecies of Dan. vii–viii, Rev. xii–xx. Cromwell's government is
greeted as a preparation for the final fulfilment of the *holy Oracles.*
After the fall of the four great kingdoms was to follow a Fifth
Monarchy, and the reign of the Saints (Dan. vii. 18) with Christ for
a thousand years (Rev. xx. 4). This is preceded in the Apocalypse by
the fall of the Great Whore ('*Hence still they sing Hosanna to the
Whore*'), and in both accounts by the destruction of the Beast
(*Winding his Horn to Kings that chase the Beast,* and *Pursues the Monster
. . . nor there secure*). The reign of God was to be preceded by the

133   in-gathering of the nations (*But Indians whom they should convert, subdue*) and in particular of the Jews. Cromwell's tacit consent to their return was confirmed at the Restoration.

134 *suspend:* at the Flood.
  Whose Saint-like Mother we did lately see: Elizabeth Cromwell died 16 November 1654, in her ninety-fourth year.

135 *Thy Brest . . . lying Prophecies:* the Protectorate was attacked by several conspiracies of Levellers and other extremists, besides those of the King's party. John Gerard, an agent of Charles II, was beheaded in July 1654 on a charge of plotting to murder Cromwell as he rode to Hampton Court.
  Our brutish fury: Cromwell driving a team of 'six great German Horses, sent him as a present by the Count of Oldenburg', upset his own coach in Hyde Park, 29 September 1654.
  yearly: celebrating the events of the year.
  purling: embroidering.

136 *Panique:* properly derived from the Pan, the god of *Natures self.*
  Center: here the earth is the centre of the universe, and the sun in the fourth sphere, to which Ptolemaic astronomy assigned it.
  But thee triumphant . . . Peoples Charioteer: Kings ii. 11–13; *Whom thou hadst left beneath with Mantle rent,* 'and he (Elisha) took hold of his own clothes, and rent them in two pieces'; *To turn the headstrong Peoples Charioteer,* 'and he cried, My father, my father, the chariot of Israel and the horsemen thereof'.

137 *Till at the Seventh time . . . wet the King:* Kings xviii, 44–6. *though fore-warn'd:* 'and he said, Go up, say unto Ahab, Prepare thy chariot and get thee down, that the rain stop thee not.'
  since: since 1649.
  But walk still middle betwixt War and Peace: the Cromwell family mottoes were *Pax quaeritur bello* and *Mors meta laborum.*
  Levell'd: the shrubs or brambles represent the Levellers.
  When Gideon so did . . . didst aw: the parallel is in Judges viii and ix. Gideon, returning from the conquest of Zeba and Zalmunna, the two kings of Midian, to Succoth, which had refused to supply his army with bread, 'took the elders of the city, and thorns of the wilderness and briers, and with them he taught the men of Succoth. And he beat down the tower of Penuel' . . . Invited to rule, he refused the headship for himself and his sons: 'The Lord shall rule over you.' The parallel is continued at *Thou with the same strength, and an Heart as plain* by way of the parable of Jotham, Gideon's son, Judges ix. 8–15.

178

Notes

138 *Corposants:* 'Marine meteors, which Portuguese mariners call the bodies of the saints. Corpos santos' (Thompson).

Eight: of Cromwell's family his wife and two sons and four daughters were living at the end of the Civil War.

Chammish: like Ham (Vulgate, Cham). The passage which follows to *Well may you act the Adam and the Eve* satirizes, probably without professing much accuracy, the religious anomalies of the middle of the seventeenth century, of which the multiplication of sects *Might muster Heresies, so one were ten* was one of the expressions. *That their new King might the fifth Scepter shake* refers to the Fifth Monarchy Men who had been preaching sedition against Cromwell: Christopher Feake and Sydrach Simpson were both imprisoned for this offence in 1654 and Feake seems to have attacked the Quakers also. *And make the World, by his Example, Quake* glances at the Quakers, whose influence was overspreading the country between the years 1648 and 1655; their early experiences, like much of the religious excitement of the time, often assumed abnormal and morbid forms *What thy Misfortune . . . to be Alcorand.*

Fall: as in falling sickness, or epilepsy, which was reputed to have accompanied Mahomet's revelations, *Oh Mahomet! now couldst thou rise again.*

their new King: may mean the still-looked-for Fifth Monarch, or some particular leader, like James Naylor, who made a messianic entry into Bristol in 1656, and was convicted thereafter of blasphemy.

Might muster Heresies, so one were ten: if one heresy could count as ten men, they would have a large army.

139 *Rant:* 'the third Sect were the *Ranters* . . . But withal, they enjoyed a Cursed Doctrine of *Libertinism*, which brought them to all abominable filthiness of Life. They taught as the *Familists*, that God regardeth not the Actions of the Outward Man, but of the Heart; and that to the Pure all things are Pure.'

Tulipant: the early and more accurate form of turban. The Quakers refused (among other 'ceremonies') to doff their hats in salute.

For prophecies fit to be Alcorand: an English translation of the Koran was published in 1649.

Munser's rest: the dregs of Munster, the city in Westphalia of which the Anabaptists took charge in 1534; they proclaimed there the New Jerusalem, abolished law, including the laws of marriage and of private property, and 'murder, polygamy and crime ran riot'.

Points: for fastening hose.

Well may you act the Adam and the Eve: Adamites of the seventeenth

179

Poems of Andrew Marvell

139 century, like those of the third, abandoned clothing in the course of their return to nature.

blacks: hangings of black cloth used at funerals.

140 *Up from the . . . Earth nor Air* (p. 141): in 1654 two fleets set sail within two months, one capturing Jamaica and the other carrying out a successful expedition against Barbary pirates.

both Wars: the Civil War and the war with Holland 1652–4.

Unless their Ships . . . Ocean breed: Hector Boethius held that the leaves of a certain tree falling into water became solan geese.

Center: See note to to page 136.

Leaguers: besieging forces.

141 *And those that have the Waters for their share:* as at the division of earth, air, and water between the sons of Cronos.

inchas'd: worked in together.

And still his Fauchion all our Knots unties: the man who loosed the Gordian knot was to be master of the world.

yearly: Cromwell had dissolved the Barebones Parliament in December 1653 and accepted the office of Protector. The succeeding Parliament was to be dissolved with a high hand in January 1655; and the first anniversary of the Protectorate (the occasion of this poem) occurred during the events which led directly to that dissolution.

142 *On the Victory obtained by Blake . . . . :* Though Cromwell's name is not mentioned in this poem, there can be no doubt that it is addressed to him, cf. especially *For your resistless . . . by their Influence.* Blake was engaged from May 1655 to August 1657 in blockading the Spanish coast and waiting to intercept treasure ships from America. On 8 September 1656 Stayner, one of his subordinates, with three ships, captured or destroyed almost the whole Plate fleet of eight vessels, and on 20 April 1656 Blake destroyed a fleet of sixteen treasure ships at Teneriffe.

143 *Casting that League off, which she held so long:* England and Spain had been at peace, since the treaty of 1630.

146 *its:* the fire's.

148 *Two Songs at the Marriage of the Lord Fauconberg and the Lady Mary Cromwell:* Thomas Belasyse (1627–1700), second Viscount Fauconberg, a kinsman of the great Lord Fairfax, married Mary Cromwell (1637–1712), third daughter of the Protector, Thursday, 19 November 1657, at Hampton Court. He became Privy Councillor and Ambassador of Charles II after the Restoration, and having joined in the invitation to the Prince of Orange at the Revolution, received an earldom in 1689.

180

Notes

149 *Anchises:* Robert Rich, grandson and heir of the Earl of Warwick, who married 11 November 1657 (one week before the marriage for which Marvell wrote these songs) Frances, Cromwell's fourth daughter, originally intended for William Dutton.

153 *A Poem upon the Death of O.C.:* Cromwell died 3 September 1658.

 To Love and Grief the fatal Writ was sign'd: Love and Grief were appointed his executioners.

 Eliza: Cromwell's second daughter, who had frequently interceded with him on behalf of Royalist prisoners.

154 *Children:* there were four, Cromwell, Henry, Oliver, and Martha. Oliver died in June 1658, thereby aggravating his mother's illness.

 A silent fire . . . tortur'd Image racks: magic against an enemy was sometimes practised by melting a wax figure in his likeness; Cromwell suffers in the suffering of his likeness Elizabeth.

155 *purple Locks:* apparently an inexact allusion to the story of Scylla the daughter of Nisus King of Megara, who, for love of Minos, cut off from her father's head the lock of purple hair on which his life depended.

 flyes: Scylla was transformed into a bird.

156 *Numbers of Men decrease with pains unknown:* days of national humiliation were decreed in May 1658 on account of the prevalent low fever.

 Nature it seem's with him would Nature vye: Nature would compete with him in natural affection.

157 *cast:* in the astrological sense, to calculate.

 Twice: at Dunbar, 3 September 1650, and at Worcester, 3 September 1651.

 Gave chase to Ligny on the Belgick Coast: on 3/13 September 1658 a Spanish force under the Prince de Ligne was defeated in Flanders by a French army with an English contingent.

 Lawrel: of victory.

158 *Who planted England . . . Indian Ore:* the capture of Dunkirk from the Spaniards (1658) and of Jamaica (1655).

 Worthy's: King Arthur was one of the Nine Worthies.

 Of that for ever Preston's field shall tell: Cromwell defeated the Scots under Hamilton near Preston 17 August 1648. *impregnable Clonmell:* because attacked unsuccessfully by Cromwell; but the Irish subsequently evacuated it (May 1650). This was the last incident in Cromwell's Irish campaign.

 Fenwick: at the battle of the Dunes 4/14 June 1658, which preceded the occupation of Dunkirk, Lieut.-Col. Roger Fenwick was mortally

158 wounded in storming a sand-hill. The day was a day of public prayer (*The sea between, yet hence his pray'r prevail'd*).

159 *Friendship, that sacred . . . house and name:* the Protector's branch of the Cromwell family was founded by his great-grandfather Richard Williams, nephew on his mother's side of Thomas Cromwell, Earl of Essex. His friendship with his uncle resulted in his being knighted and in his adoption of the surname Cromwell.

But within one . . . extended unto all: but while friendship attaches to one object, Cromwell's '*tendernesse extended unto all*'.

160 *Francisca:* Cromwell's youngest daughter Frances, married to Robert Rich in 1657. She afterwards married Sir John Russell, and died in 1721.

162 *Richard:* Richard Cromwell (1626–1712) was proclaimed Protector on the day of his father's death, but resigned the title in April 1659.

163 *On Mr Milton's Paradise Lost:* The second edition (1674) of *Paradise Lost* is introduced by two poems, one in Latin by S(amuel) B(arrow), M.D., and these lines by Marvell (signed A.M.) which immediately precede Milton's foreword on 'The Verse'.

Sampson: Samson Agonistes had first appeared with *Paradise Regained*, in 1671.

some less skilful hand: a reference to Dryden, whose *The State of Innocence, and Fall of Man* was an operatic version of Milton's poem.

164 *Bird nam'd from that Paradise:* Birds of Paradise were so named by the Dutch voyagers in allusion to the brilliancy of their plumage, and to the current belief that, possessing neither wings nor feet, they passed their lives in the air, sustained on their ample plumes, resting only at long intervals suspended from the branches of lofty trees by the wire-like feathers of the tail, and drawing their food 'from the dews of heaven and the nectar of flowers'. Marvell, however, here gives them wings.

Town-Bays: Dryden appears in Buckingham's *Rehearsal* (1672) in the character of Bayes.

Points: for fastening hose. They were tasselled ('bushy') or tagged (like modern shoelaces). The 'bushy' fancies are crushed into the tag and lose their quality and character.